Bury St Edmunds Memories

MARTYN TAYLOR

AMBERLEY

Acknowledgements

To all of the contributors, I would like to say a big thank you for giving up your time and also bringing to light those long-lost photographs that have helped to 'put the meat on the bones' of your memories, especially Anglia Newspapers, Bedfords, Paul Burgess, David Emerson, Nigel Finch and Richard Green and also to Amberley Publishing for giving me the opportunity to pursue what has been a labour of love. Last but not least, my ever-patient wife Sandie whose scrutiny of my efforts is so much appreciated. I would like to dedicate this book to Kingsley Curtis and Gwen Roberts who passed away in 2015.

First published 2015

Amberley Publishing
The Hill, Stroud
Gloucestershire, GL5 4EP

www.amberley-books.com

British Library Cataloguing in Publication Data.
A catalogue record for this book is available from the British Library.

ISBN 978 1 4456 4497 4 (print)
ISBN 978 1 4456 4517 9 (ebook)

Typesetting and Origination by Amberley Publishing.
Printed in the UK.

Contents

Introduction

Obviously, Bury has changed, over the past 100 years, new shops, roads and housing, new people, new memories. Life in bygone years was set at a more sedate pace without the hustle and bustle of today and there was little in the way of luxuries, the austerity of the world wars saw to that. Many people have reflected how hard life was for their families. It is amazing how much certain places of education such as The Silver Jubilee Schools played in formulating much of the lives of Bury people. Today, the archive of oral history is just as important as the written word; however, when someone passes away, those untold memories are lost forever. As the 'old grey matter' dims so does the ability to recall events that may not have had that momentous effect on a person's life but did add to their character. I have been extremely lucky to tap into that reservoir of stored knowledge of some of the residents of Bury St Edmunds who can remember their childhood, school and working life, pastimes, conflicts, etc. What it has also shown me is what you put into life so you take out. It is often said that fate plays a strange hand when dealing out the cards of fortune. I, like the many people who have contributed to this book, consider that we are extremely fortunate to have grown up in such a wonderful place as Bury St Edmunds. Some may have moved away but ultimately returned, and others are part of ongoing generations who have lived here all their lives. There are even reminisces of outsiders who have become insiders, almost locals. It is all these lives that are explored within these pages. Monetary terms are expressed predecimalisation. All the recollections are the contributors, and consequently, the information supplied is as true as they have remembered them.

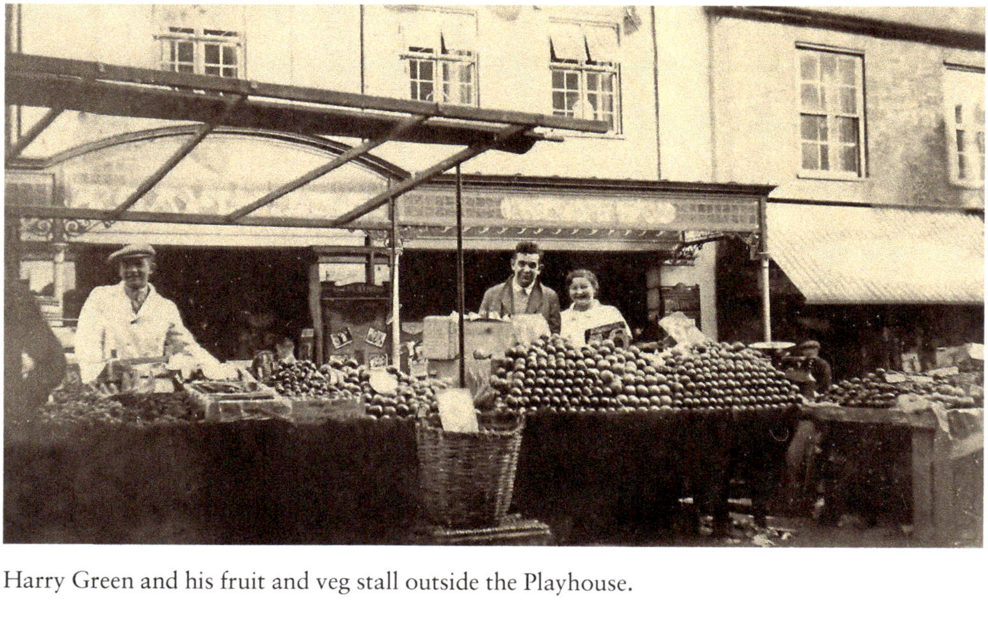

Harry Green and his fruit and veg stall outside the Playhouse.

Childhood

Philip Road

One of my earliest memories as a young child was when Philip Road was extended. My father, Ivan Frost, had purchased the then last bungalow on the north side in 1939 for £450. A hawthorn hedge formed the boundary with open fields the other side. My dad told me that prisoners of war laid out the roads on the Mildenhall Estate soon after 1946. Philip Road was unmade then, and I used to get filthy playing in the dusty road as it was safe with no through traffic. However, I used to have a change of clothes everyday – something that displeased my mother. In the early 1950s, the council bulldozed the hedge down and made my parents and the neighbours stump up £120 each to surface the road that now became a through road to the rest of the estate; this made them very angry.

Jennifer Hatton née Frost (born 1946).

The Piggy Market

Growing up in Bury was wonderful as we could go about without a care in the world. I liked going to the cattle market and loved the smell of the pigs. Sometimes, I would see them after taking rabbit skins to Brahams in Risbygate Street. I used to go into Croasdales Chemists and staring for ages at the beautiful coloured glass bottles especially the blue ones that fascinated me. I never did know what they had in them. Mr Croasdale who shuffled along was a proper gentleman. I learnt to swim up at the open-air swimming pool on the playfields. I can also remember going down to the Abbey Gardens dancing around a maypole on 1 May with peacocks strutting about. On Saturday mornings, like loads of other children, I used to go to the Odeon cinema that cost *6d*. When my son was very small, we always went into town via the pig market something that kids miss out on today.

Shirley Pattle née Wraight (born 1940).

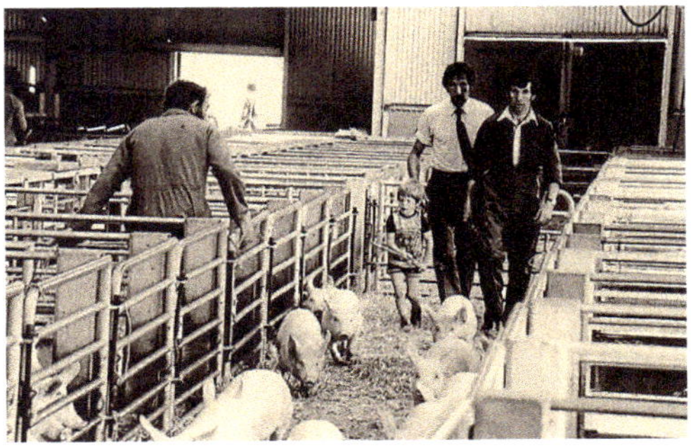

Bury's livestock market closed in 1998, the end of an era.

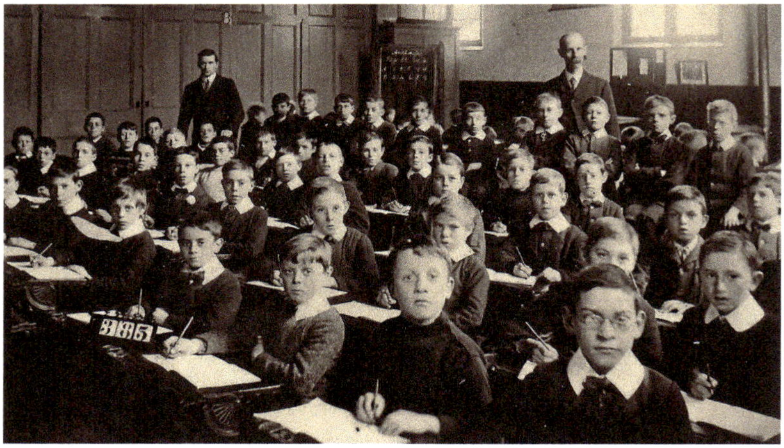

The main classroom in the Guildhall Feoffment School, *c.* 1912.

The Trunk

My father Joseph Bruton became landlord of the Elephant & Castle also known as the Trunk after my grandmother Ellen Bruton finished, Greene King's oldest serving landlady! I was bullied at St Peters School so never went to the Guildhall Feoffment where my father had been, instead going to St Edmundsbury – I never did like school. When I was around sixteen, I used to open up the Trunk's back door early so some of the regulars could get a bottle of beer, and they drunk it in the cart lodge. They worked at places like Bobys, the Brewery and Hand Laundry; obviously, some had to have a drink to get them going! Father used to go up to the market a few weeks before Christmas to buy turkeys and some geese to fatten them up for the table. They were kept in our yard at the back. The trouble was they wouldn't let anyone into the yard with all their hissing and that! Father had a pet tortoise called Billy; it was an ancient creature with his name painted on its shell. If it wandered up St Andrew's Street, somebody would always bring it back as it never got very far! One winter, it was very mild in February, and Billy woke up from hibernation; the trouble was a cold snap soon followed, and the poor old thing must have frozen to death. Father was very upset about it.

Roger Bruton (born 1944).

Incarceration

I was nearly eleven when I got a job at the Maltings up by the 'Chalks'. I had to prick the holes of a twelve-inch square perforated sheet where grain went through. Using one 'pricker' took me ages, but some clever clogs had wooden blocks with nails knocked through which did it a lot quicker. Now I think of it, my one penny for doing each sheet was underage slavery! I was incarcerated in the Grammar School (that's what it felt like), a cold place of education, it was particularly bad during the harsh winter of 1947.

Gerald 'Gerry' Travers (born 1935).

Swimming with Frogs

We used to go for long walks when we lived on the Priors; there were open fields where the Horringer Court Estate now is. When we went to Sunday school at St Peters church, our teacher Mrs Ridley gave us wine gums, and they were lovely. We used to play on the old First World War tank in the Abbey Gardens, and the park keeper Mr Frost had a really loud voice and would shout at us if we were up to no good. I wonder whatever happened to that tank. There was a bandstand in the park as we called it, and they used to play really nice music every Sunday. One of the funniest things I recall is swimming among frogs that got into the Brewery swimming baths in Maynewater Lane!

Betty Woodward née Ransome (born 1921).
Joan Horsham née Ransome (born 1923).

Travelling down Eastgate Street

My father Maurice Wilson kept the post office in Eastgate Street. Two other shops were a greengrocers run by Arthur Pollard with Charlie Allen's bike shop next door. Charlie was once asked to ride his Penny Farthing bike from the top of Eastgate Street as fast as he could. He took on the challenge, and it was reckoned he was travelling at around 25 mph by the time he got to the railway bridge (now A14 flyover). He just managed to stop falling off. In the terrible winter of 1963, I saw something amazing: two people came down Eastgate Street on skis!

Grenville Wilson (born 1949).

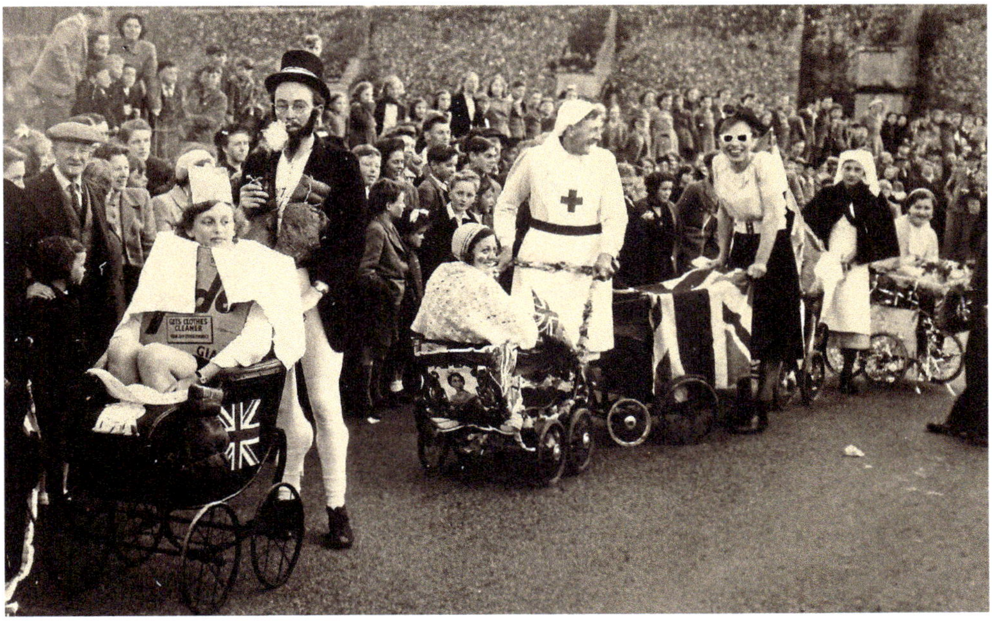

Maurice Wilson wearing the top hat in Eastgate Street's Coronation pram race.

Road Games

Abbot Road used to finish at the Perry Barn where there was the Home Guard Club, a facility founded by 'Monty' Banks during the Second World War. I was born at No. 5 Abbot Road (it was renumbered 10 in 1957). My mother was a good cook, honest and simple; stew and dumplings, steam puddings and rabbit pie, etc. Dad worked at the sugar beet factory and would acquire a brace for five bob from the pest control officer there. We only had a coal fire in the living room, so it wasn't uncommon to have ice inside on the bedroom windows. Every so often I used to push a barrow down to Whitmore's timber yard in Fornham Road during the winter to collect logs for the fire. I was told to give the old boy who filled the barrow a piece of chewing gum so he would put extra logs in! It was easy going down the hills with the barrow empty, but the return to home was very hard! Opposite our home, a member of the wealthy Ridley family lived in a splendid house, when built around 1906, it was called 'Fairyland'. It had a colonial style veranda overlooking a wood. This was known to us kids who played in it as 'Old Ma Ridley's Wood'. Very little traffic used the road, and we played rounders and tennis in the street. Occasionally, delivery men such as Bluett's fruit and veg van or Childs' the baker's horse-drawn float would interrupt the game.

Martyn Taylor (born 1950).

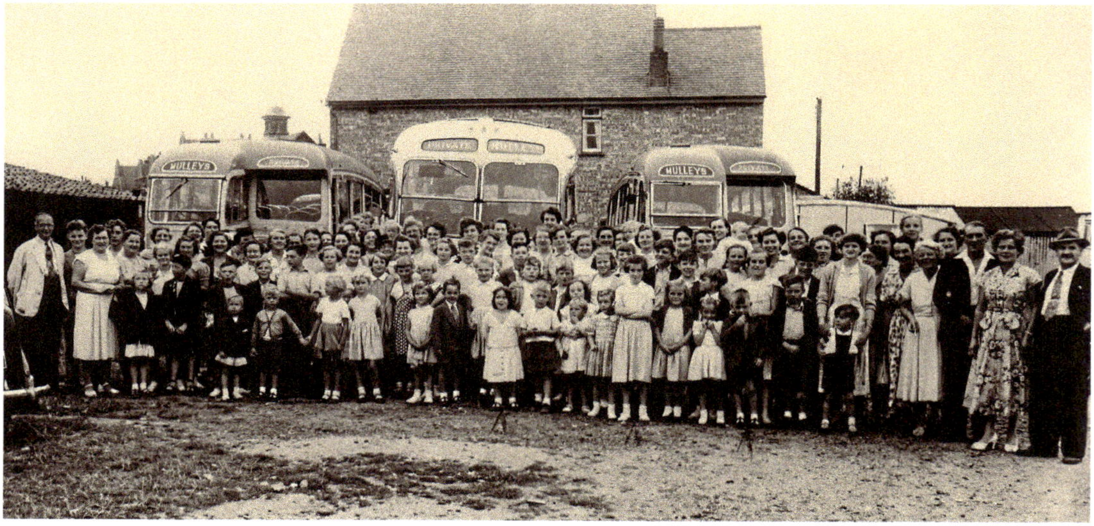

The Priors Inn trip to Walton on the Naze in 1955; the author is the third child from the right.

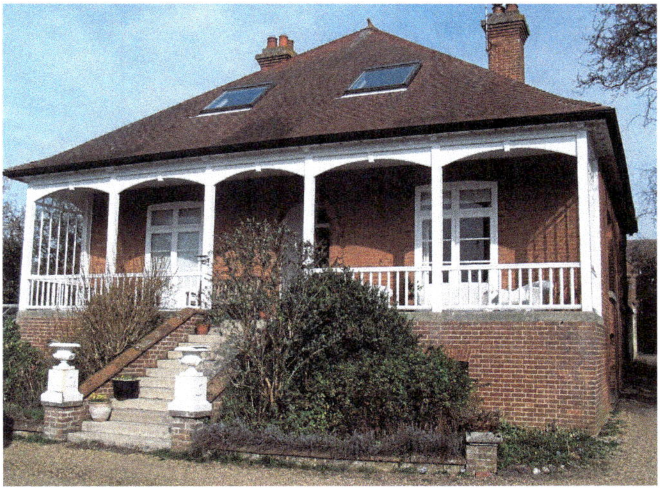

The former 'Fairyland', once the home of Mrs Ridley.

Smelly Stuff

One Christmas, dad was stuffing a chicken, and after sewing it up, mum asked where the needle was. She thought he had left it inside the bird and he had to undo all his handiwork. She then found it in the sewing box where he had put it; boy was the air blue for a while after that. When older, me and a load of my mates were down in Old Man Ridleys Wood when she appeared holding a gun, she scared the living daylights out of us. On running out of the wood, I was smacked in the face by a branch. My face came up like a balloon so I had to go to hospital and was off school for weeks after. One day, I went with my Aunt Elsie from my home on the Priors down to Westley Road near the junction with Gainsborough Road. There was an orchard here where pigs were kept. We wheeled a barrow load of vegetable peelings to feed them. I went off to get some apples but fell into a disused well full of a smelly black liquid that came from the pigs! I was wheeled home in the barrow absolutely stinking!

Carol Waters (born 1945).

Mucking About?

I was brought up in Springfield Road, a very friendly neighbourhood, and we played games like Stones and Jacks. You could also roam about all over the place as when Roger, my brother, and I did when we were bought new bikes by our father. I can remember dancing around a maypole at the St Edmundsbury school; it had to be done properly so the ribbons created the right pattern. When I was around twelve, I went with friends to Doreen Nice's stables in Risbygate Street to help muck out in exchange for pony rides. One day while there I stood on a rake that flew up and knocked me out cold! Something I always enjoyed was the Christmas get-together with my cousins at Brayfields, the Butchers.

Rosemary Rayson née Vickers (born 1948).

Going About

My maternal grandfather, Bob Hopwood, acquired an existing butchers shop in St John's Street when he came out of the army after the Second World War. Bob had been involved in the Nuremberg trials and met Joanna, an Austrian, who became his wife; she was an interpreter. My mother and father moved around Bury as his jobs changed, initially at No. 3, Lower Baxter Street, which was demolished to make way for the Borough Offices extension in 1965. While this was being built, the family lived in Ridley Road later returning to a purpose-built flat. My younger brother Nick and I used to get up to all sorts of mischief here especially at weekends when no one was about, like riding our bikes in the corridors. The nearby Abbey Gardens was our playground. As time progressed, we would spend time up on the old railway line near to where the cycle bridge to Moreton Hall is today. Often we ventured into the old chalk caves at the top of Eastgate Street and down to the Showmans site off Rushbrook Lane. Collecting up Coca-Cola bottles and returning them for their deposits was one way we earned a few bob. Our Saturdays were spent at the pictures at the Odeon and then Purdys restaurant with their wonderful sausage rolls and meeting up with friends who came into Bury on a bus. As I got older, I worked on the market opposite 18 Plus (Body Shop there now) selling printed T-shirts and dresses for the guy who owned Annabel Togs in Abbeygate Street, often popping into the Suffolk Hotel for refreshments! After my family moved to No. 9, Great Churchyard, it meant cutting through there at different times. After dark when I was working part-time in the Roaring Twenties restaurant on Angel Hill, it was a bit creepy. I am sure there was an unusual presence at times, your mind sees what you think you should see, but you are not totally convinced what it is, I don't know? I was around seventeen, and there was a lot more about the town to do then, Rollerbury, events at the Corn Exchange and school friends with local discos. After I got my O and A levels, I went to college and made a career in marketing but returned to the Bury I love though travelling the world as and when.

Colin Taylor (born 1957).

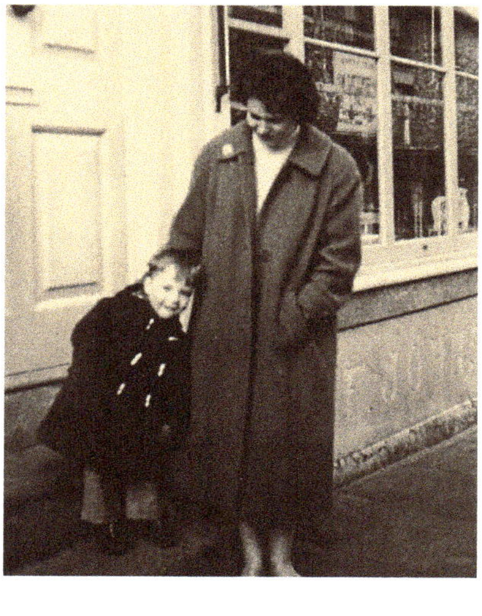

Colin Taylor with his mother Pauline in St John's Street.

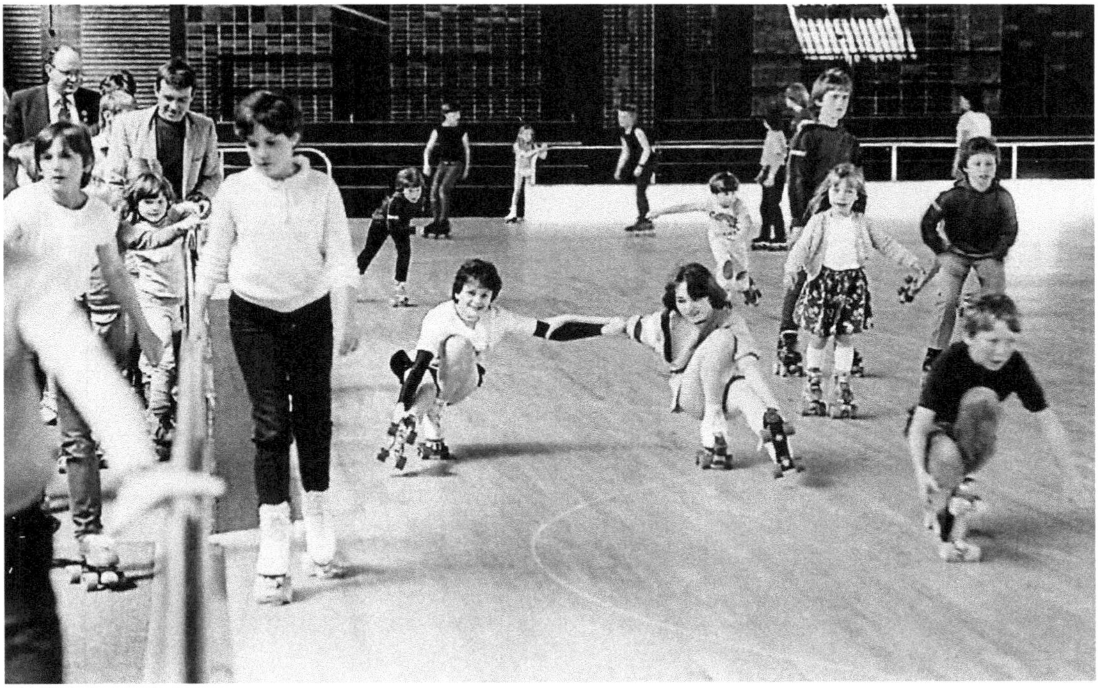

The once-popular Rollerbury.

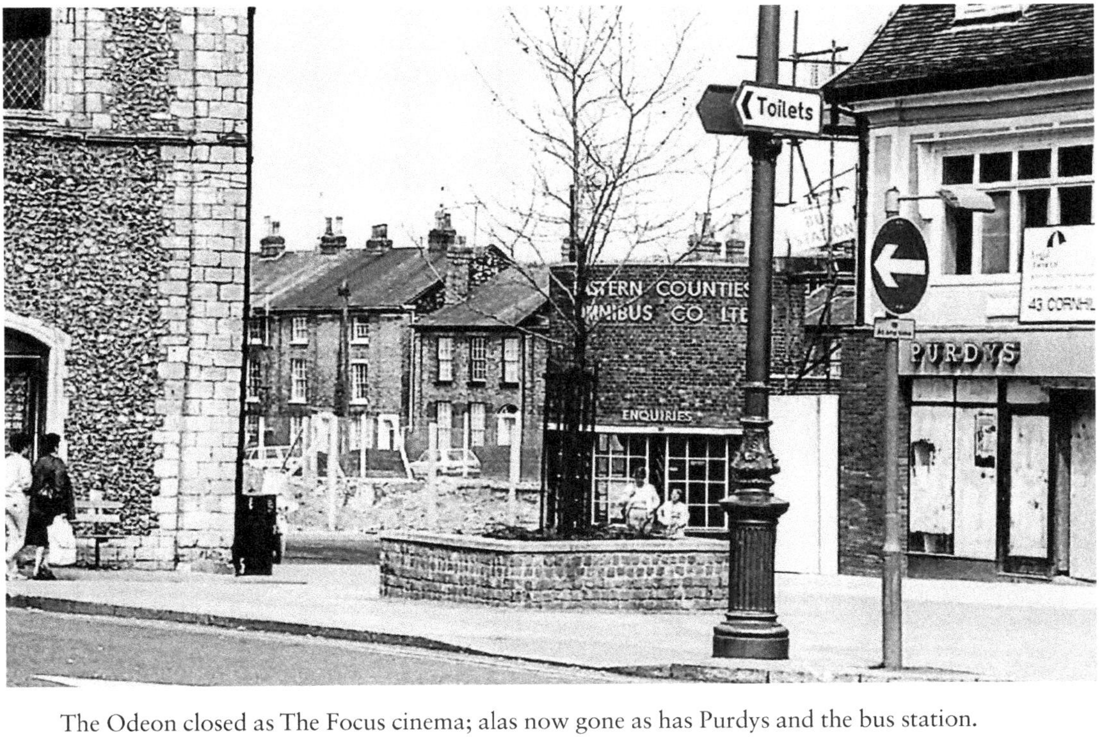

The Odeon closed as The Focus cinema; alas now gone as has Purdys and the bus station.

Prospects

The family home was at No. 41, Prospect Row, now gone. We shared the rear outside water tap with three other houses in the terrace. Likewise, the toilet at the bottom of the garden was shared with next door. I hated going up there in the dark with a candle because nine times out of ten the wind would blow it out. When I was small, a lorry drove into our house, and we had to live at No. 8, while the house was done up. As children, we sat on the corner of Prospect Row, taking car numbers down because we were told the police would give us some money if you got lots. It wasn't flippin' true of course, and it took ages for a car to pass by! I played with my friends in the street, games like hopscotch, marbles and skipping with a rope right across the road, and we would go tadpole and stickleback fishing down by the Butts; we made our own entertainment, no television then! Mum and dad used to take us on pub outings with the Butchers Arms and the Duke of Wellington, which was more or less opposite our house. The outings were looked upon as the only holidays we were likely to get! As my dad's job on the council wasn't well paid, and my mum used to have a couple of cleaning jobs. One of them was at Lloyds Bank, and I used to help her by mixing up the ink powder with water and filling the inkwells.

Sheila Collins née Walden (born 1937).

Magazines

As a youngster, I loved playing with Meccano sets. One Christmas, I was lucky enough to be given a number six Meccano set, and I added gear wheels and stuff like that allowing me to spend hours playing with it. We had moved from our home in Hospital Road to a large house in St Andrew's St South called Pencoed, Welsh for 'Top of the Wood'. The neighbour produced the *Meccano* magazine that I loved. They had inherited, at the bottom of the garden, a powder magazine that the former owner, gunsmith Mr Scotcher, had constructed for his products. Still written in chalk on the door was 'remove boots and put galoshes on!'

Ted Ashton (born 1941).

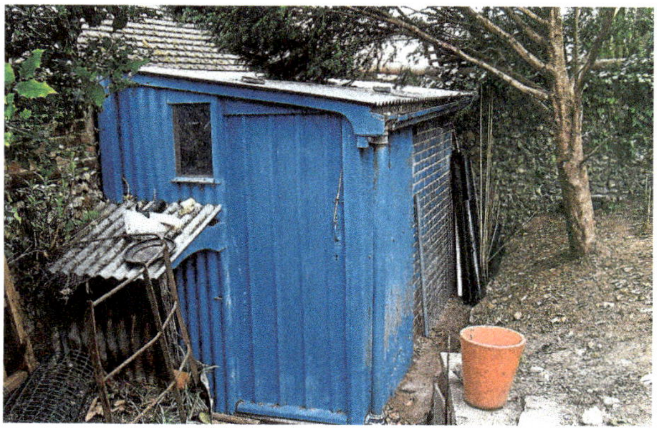

This was once the black powder magazine of Mr Scotcher, gunsmith.

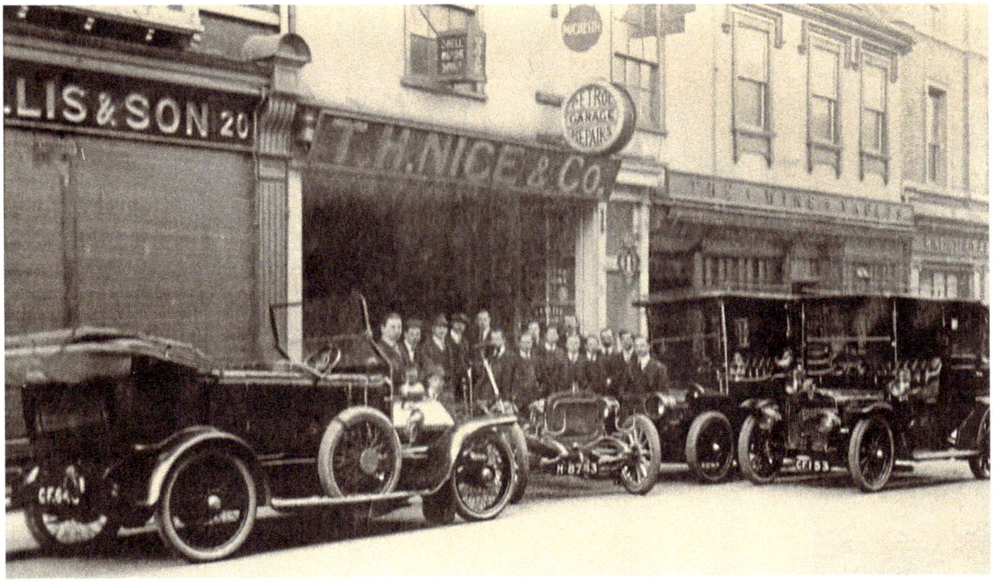

The Abbeygate street garage of T. H. Nice.

EMU

My father was Marcus Bird, a doctor at the old hospital, a local magistrate, and was well respected. He eventually went into private practice as a GP with his father-in-law, Dr Joe Hinnell, at No. 62, Garland Street. I moved there with my parents in 1934. I went to Portland House School in Guildhall Street run by two sisters the Misses Underwood; one was called Polly and the other Edith. No one knew her middle name, but it began with an M as she always signed herself as EMU! They were very good teachers. One thing that has stayed with me throughout my life is that I consider myself good at spelling something that was installed by them. When I was eight years old, I was packed off to boarding school as most professional person's children were then. In 1946, I got a scholarship to Oundle School which paid for one term; the annual fees were £300 per annum, a lot of money in those days. In the school holidays, I came back home to Bury; it was wonderful going down Abbeygate Street, as the shops then were independently run and owned. One particular shop I liked was Harpers Music Salon on the corner with Lower Baxter Street run by Miss Marjory Wormald. Mr Alec Burgess had his butchers shop next door, proper old-fashioned butchers that had smashing pork pies. Near to this was Nice's Garage; it had a petrol pump where a chap in a long brown coat would come out and fill your petrol tank. On the corner with Higher Baxter Street was Dunns Restaurant owned by Ronnie Wilcox, and he was always smartly dressed. He later became a captain in the Home Guard. On the other side of the street was J. T. Fields corsetier shop, and its owner used to come outside of the shop virtually every hour to survey the street up and down. It was said he suffered from claustrophobia.

Jos Bird (born 1933).

The Circus Comes to Town

Thomas Pike, my father, was manager of the gas showroom in the Traverse, and my mum, Gladys, was a window dresser for Woolworths. I was born in Risbygate Street near the Barracks, and my first school, Victoria Infants, had a big 'tortoise stove' that had a fireguard around; we used to hang our wet clothes on it when it was raining. On Coronation Day, all we kids went up to Angel Hill where we were given a coronation mug and a small cardboard box with a sandwich, sausage roll and a bun in. When I was around thirteen, dad took me to the railway station to see the circus come off the train, the elephants used to walk through the town, and people came out of their doors with a bucket and shovel to collect the necessary for their rose beds! Another time, he took me up to the railway crossing on Beetons Footpath to see the Flying Scotsman go by.

Shirley Ransome née Pike (born 1942).

Feeding Fish

I was born at No. 4, Chalk Road; the B&Q carpark is there now. We then moved to Cannon Street, dad was in the Royal Air Force (RAF), and mum used to work on fields out in the fens; she got picked up by a van daily. Times were hard then, but do you know what, we never locked our doors. Perhaps it was because we never had anything worth stealing! You couldn't do that today. I used to go down to the gasworks and get some coke for the fire, the workers there had big goldfish in the cooling tanks, and we were allowed to feed them. I went to the Railway Mission Room on Sundays, Quakers on Wednesday and the Salvation Army on Fridays. Not that I was religious or anything like that, it was because they took us out on outings, and as there was no car in the family, they were like holidays for us kids!

Wendy Wells née Smith (born 1945).

Proper Printers

My father, Tom Pawsey, worked in the family printing firm in Hatter Street from the age of fifteen; they produced really nice postcards among other stuff. My grandfather had started the business. I had three sisters, and when I was young and dad used to drive us to the seaside, I felt very privileged. My mum, Lizzie, made a great big apple turnover to take along. I left the Jubilee School aged fourteen and went to work after the war in the public library in the School of Art as a librarian (Harriets Tea Rooms 2015), leaving when I married in 1952. In my spare time, I used to help out selling the yellow-covered almanacs, which Pawseys were famous for.

Gwen Roberts née Pawsey (born 1931).

Greengrocery

Harry Green, my father, purchased a shop on the corner of St Andrew's St South and Risbygate Street, just before I was born in a nursing home at No. 1, Northgate Street. At just over four years old, I attended St Louis Convent School, one of only nine boys there. During the war, mother woke me up one night when a doodlebug went over, very strange that. I also remember dad going up to Westley to get apples in a Commer lorry, and a funny thing happened when an American soldier stopped me once near our shop and gave me an apple; obviously, he never knew what dad did. I liked going to the cinema especially the Playhouse. Once at a showing there of Romeo and Juliet at the point where she says 'Romeo, Romeo wherefore art thou Romeo' somebody shouted out 'he's in the bush', everybody roared with laughter! After going to St Edmundsbury School, I went to the Silver Jubilee. I didn't much like sports – I've always thought if you can't do something well there's no point in doing it. I remember music teacher 'Taffy' Evans and Archie Candler the science teacher. He would put you right if you messed about! I was quite good at technical drawing and was very surprised to see two of my architectural sketches still on the wall when I went back to the school ten years after I left. About leaving, my father was asked by a careers master what I was going to do. Dad said, 'He'd go in the family business'. When father was asked what that was then, he replied, 'Greengrocers'. The master just said, 'Well, that's that sorted'. I ran the business until 1998, the last proper greengrocers in Bury.

Richard Green (born 1939).

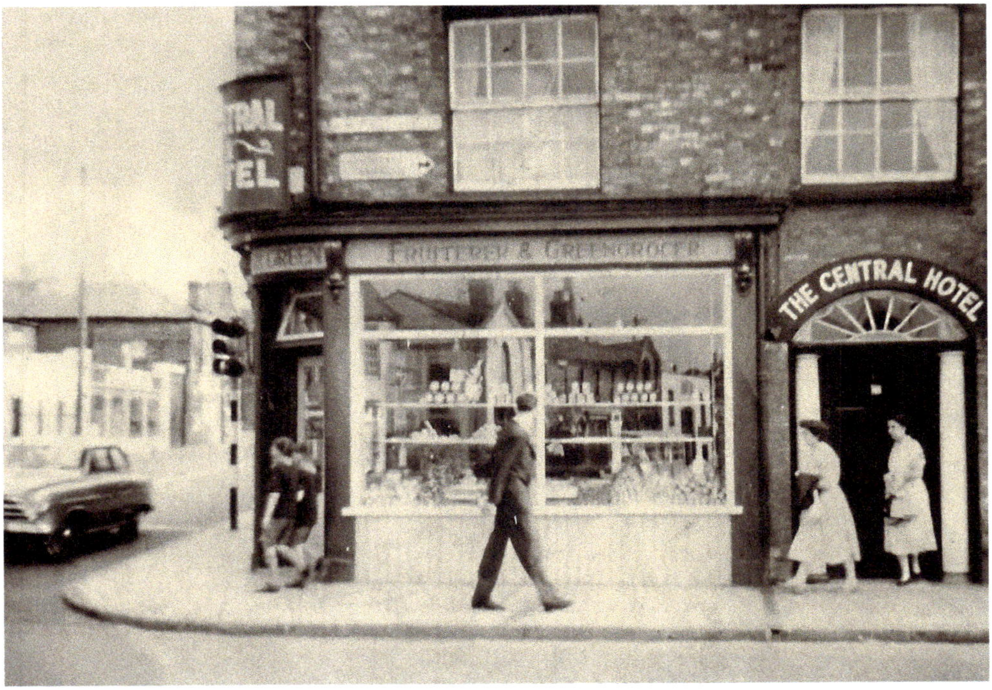

The last greengrocers in Bury St Edmunds.

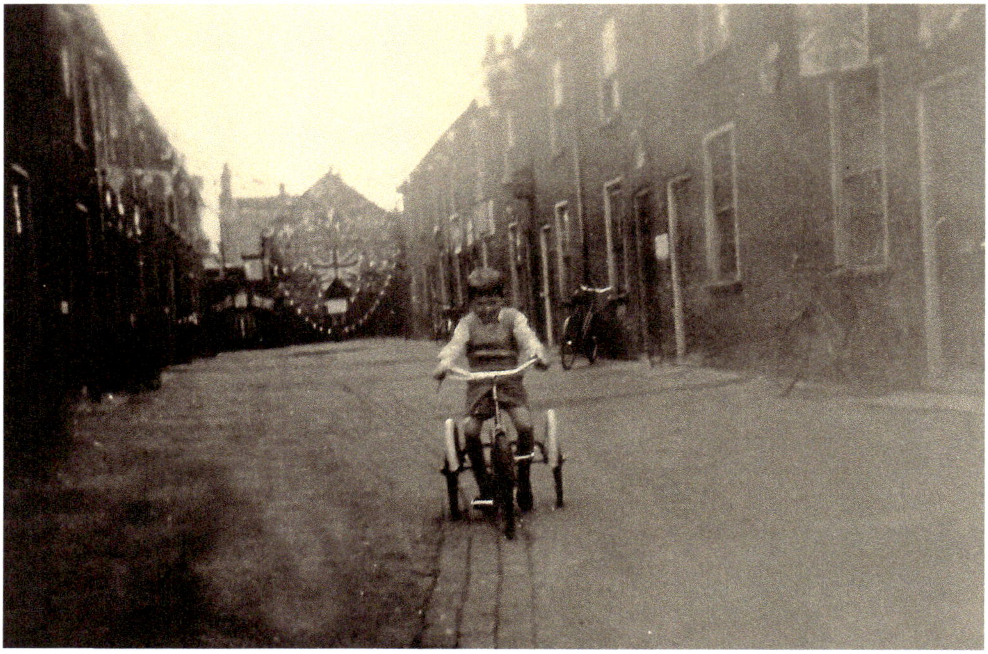

David Hoggett in the now demolished St Edmunds Place, decorated for the Coronation in 1953.

Earning Coppers

St Edmunds Place was a cul-de-sac with a small memorial at one end to men from there that died in the First World War. Our house only had two bedrooms for us all. The place opened onto Cannon Square; Frewer's bakery, Philips' hairdressers, Smith's grocery shop, Hibbets fish and chip shop and St Edmunds Head also known as the Cannon Brewery were all here. I was around ten when I started earning pennies by running errands for Brayfields and Boughtons, both butchers. However, my biggest earner was collecting the Christmas club money from around seven houses on a Monday night. The Cannon ran it all year long, and I got the interest from it! The money came in handy for the pictures, watching Bury Town and getting the Green 'Un'. I also collected beer and Vimto bottles to get back their deposits. With a couple of mates, I would go carol singing sometimes outside the pubs, but the landlord of the Red Lion made us sing inside, a hat passed round for our efforts. In the summer, I helped mum fruit picking, but always ate more than I picked! I liked going with her to the railway station to see the animals come off the train and herded up St Andrew's Street to the market, also going down to the Abbey gardens to see the brass band play there – that led me to play the bugle in the Boys' Brigade. One thing you had to do in September was to start building your bonfire ready for Guy Fawkes Night, the bigger the better. In those days nearly all the kids went to Sunday school, I went to the Lathbury Institute in Church Row. Who would ever have thought I would help convert it into a private house fifty years later when I was a bricklayer!

David Hoggett (born 1947).

Long Trousers

My father, William Colson, was one of a line of publicans going back a hundred years. My first two years were at his pub, The Three Horseshoes in Northgate Street, we then moved to the Spread Eagle. Some of the things I can remember about times then were the Suffolk Punch horses belonging to the Corporation being on the nearby water meadows. They were brought there by Mr Bradley; on release, they ran about like youngsters. We would often be given rides on them. As we did on Pam Banks Shetland pony, we used to tease, it but one day, it got its own back when it stood on my foot; it brought tears to my eyes! Once I was swinging on a rope tied to one of the willow trees that straddled the Linnet, I was wearing my first pair of long worsted trousers. However, the rope broke plunging me into the river. A friend who lived nearby helped wash the mud off them, but I was found out when mother discovered that the dye had run on them. I got a clip around the ear for my trouble and went back into short trousers for a while.

Ron Colson (born 1929).

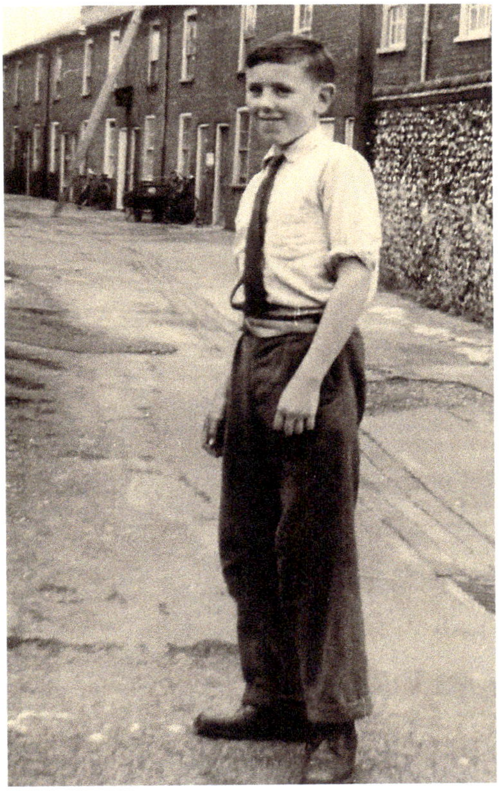

David Hoggett, aged thirteen, in long trousers!

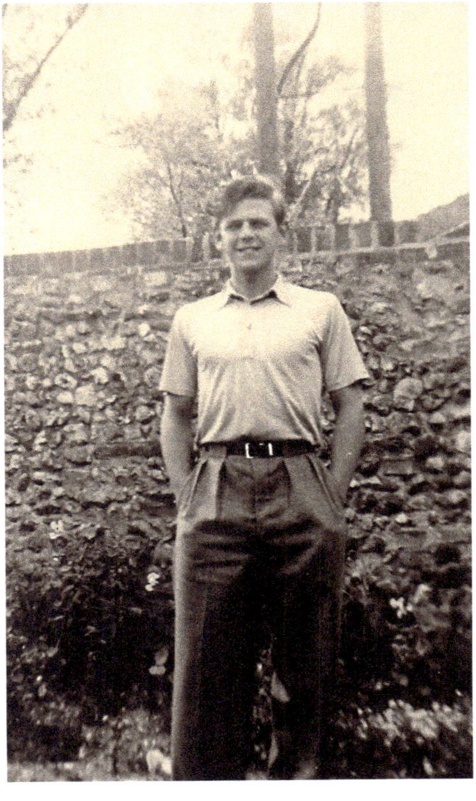

Ron Colson in long trousers!

Choirs and Cubs

I went to St Edmundsbury School because my parents wanted me to join St Mary's church choir. Its organist and choirmaster, Norman Jones, was a teacher there. I really enjoyed singing in the choir as it was the only real talent you could say I possessed. Once I was even chosen to sing in St Paul's Cathedral! Carol singing was carried out by the choir around the hotels in Bury; we were joined by the adult choristers then. We once sang in the masonic lodge in Churchgate Street, you could cut the tobacco smoke with a knife as it was that thick. I was also in the 6th Bury Cubs, and Miss Hammond was in charge. We met in St Mary's House in Whiting Street; my father and others later helped with the construction of a proper scouts headquarters in Hog Lane. Spending weekend camp up on Hardwick Heath was very enjoyable as was the time the pack biked over to Mundford for Summer Camp in 1959, something you wouldn't even think of doing now!

Royston Crack (born 1946).

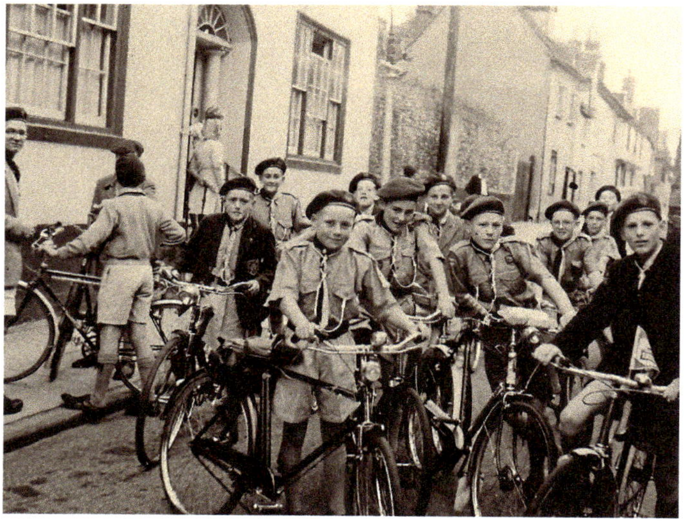

6th Bury Cubs in Whiting Street preparing to leave for Camp in 1959.

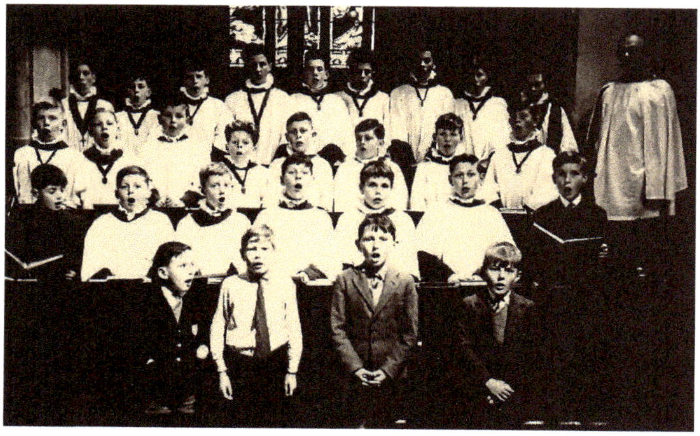

Royston Crack at rear on the left, St Mary's Choir 1958.

What's in a name?

When I was christened in St Mary's, the vicar asked for the names I was to be given. However, when he found out I wasn't to be given a middle name, he said, 'Could I give him mine?' Well, father knew his name was Thomas and agreed thinking it was to be this but guess what, we ended up with matching middle names. His full name being Thomas Brocas Waters!

Percy Brocas Taylor (born 1908).

Meeting Father

I was three months old when my father went off to France; he was involved in Dunkirk. We lived in one of seven houses in Bakers Lane just off Southgate Street, having one tap between us all. When I was five, my mother got a telegram to say father was coming home. The next day, at seven in the morning, I looked out of the window and saw a man in uniform standing there, and it is the first time I can recall seeing my father. I was at Eastgate Infants School when there was terrible flooding in 1947, and we were ferried across by army lorries! Something that sticks in my mind was an old stove there that had to have the flue swept now and again; we were taken out for a walk when the sweep came. When rationing finished, there were queues of us outside Turvey's tobacconist and sweet shop round the corner in Southgate Street. Just before I left school at fifteen, I delivered paraffin for Mr Pryke of Churchgate Street, and he sold all sorts of stuff including rolls of lino that stood outside his shop.

Neville Waller (born 1939).

In Isolation

I was born in Hollow Road, my father, Fred Reynolds, was a timber merchant who had been born at No. 8, The Broadway in Eastgate Street. His family had lived there since the 1840s; on the death of my father, I inherited the house and still have it. My first school was at St Louis Convent, and when I was seven, I had a really bad fall severely damaging one of my knees. I was in hospital for long periods of time. While here Italian prisoners of war (POWs) used to bring the laundry to the wards unfortunately for me and several others, I contracted diphtheria probably from them which meant the ward was put under quarantine. My visiting parents could only look at me through a porthole window in the door! I ended up in an isolation sanatorium in Sicklesmere Road for six weeks. Even my poor teddy had to be fumigated! My mother, who was a teacher, then taught me at home for two years before I went to The East Anglian Girls' School. I always remember listening to Dick Barton on the wireless, tuning in at 6.45 p.m. every night, don't forget there was no television (TV) in those days.

Bridget James née Reynolds (born 1936).

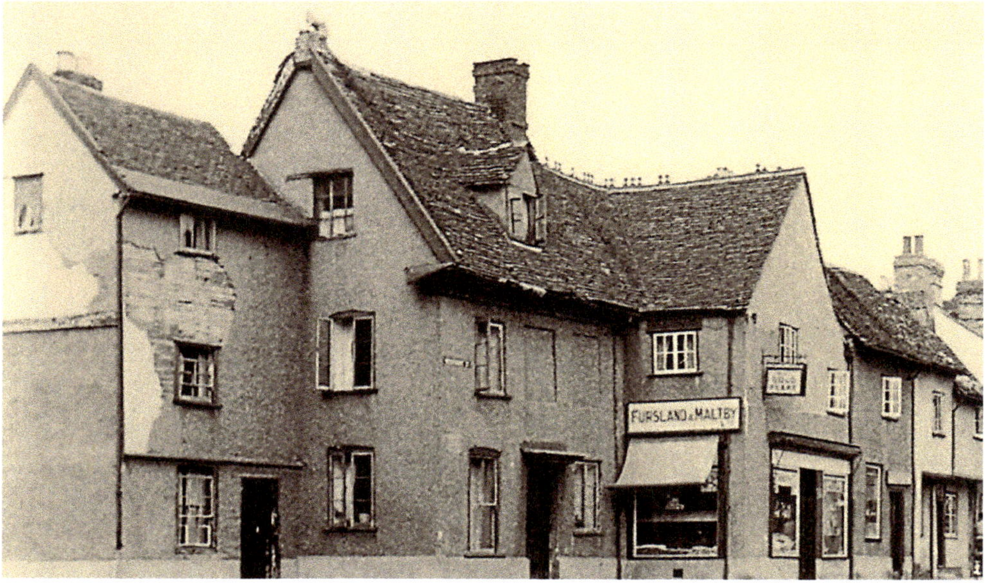

Corner of Westgate Street and St Andrew's St South AKA Hellfire Corner.

Hellfire Corner

I lived at No. 31, Westgate Street till I was sixteen years old. Now sadly demolished, the house was old with a stone ram on the top and beams inside. We only had gas mantles to see by, no inside water and a shared outside toilet! When the farmers brought their cattle up Out Westgate for market, we would run out of our backyard onto the 'Bungy', to see them; this was a piece of sloping ground along the rear of the British Legion. Opposite this was a blacksmiths forge, and we would watch the horses being shod. In the mornings, the Corporation's heavy horses came up the west from Holywater Meadows to their yard in Kings Road, and they were taken back again at 5.30 p.m. We had a 'midnight coalman', he would have candles in lamps at the back of his dray. Also Mr Freeman, a rag and bone man bought our rabbit skins for *6d*, just enough for the cinema! Several shops on Westgate Street included Fursland and Maltby, they had lovely fruit, and the man in there would sell you some for a penny; next door was a barber called Freddie Caldwell. When they pulled his place down, they took the mirrors out and put them in the Theatre Royal. Then, there was this nice sweet shop; the man who had it – 'Darkie' Double – ran a bookies around the back, something that wasn't allowed in those days. Sometimes an old tramp would knock on our door for some water to put it in his old tin can as he made his way up to the 'Spike', the workhouse in Mill Road; it later became St Mary's Geriatric Hospital. They used to give him an old straw mattress to sleep on. Another old character who lived at the top of Out Westgate was 'Muggy' Warren; he wore wellington boots all the time. Most days he would walk to Great Whelnetham church to keep an eye on it, but he never spoke a word! As children, we played a lot up on Hardwick Heath and often saw the POWs marching about.

Barbara Clements née Curry (born 1936).

Barrow Boy

I was born in No. 39, Prospect Row that was once thought to be a pub. When I was growing up, canal barges used to come out of Bobys in King's Road on Pickfords low-loaders going down to meet the A45 at the back of Everards Hotel in St Andrew's St South. They had a hell of a job to get round the corner. Bobys used to do a lot of work on these barges. Council dustcarts used to deliver their rubbish via Prospect Row to the incinerator on the Playfields. Occasionally, a steeplejack would arrive and put his ladder against the incinerator chimney and haul himself up on the metal bands around the bricks to inspect it. When I was around eleven, I worked on Bury fruit market on Wednesdays and Saturdays but also worked some Sundays on Angel Hill off a London-style barrow that was stored in the White Lion yard. I would bring orange boxes home for firewood.

Reg Cowlin (born 1948).

A Sad Story

We lived in Eastgate Street, and my mother, Violet, used to take in lodgers, mainly Irish who came over to work at the sugar beet factory during the campaign. My father, Bertie worked there as well, he was sadly killed at the age of thirty-five when a passing car knocked him down, while he was being dropped off home by a sugar beet lorry. In those days, the dead were laid out in a coffin in the front room so people could pay their last respects, my dad was.

Bertie Willingham (born 1930).

A Clip Around the Ear

Where the shops at Stamford Court are now (2015), there used to be two lovely old flint cottages with candy twist chimneys. Across the way stood Mothersoles laundry, it was in the garden of No. 18, Horringer Road and was basically a brick shed overlooking the Linnet. There was this bloke that used to hang around, and we called him the 'poacher' as he always had a brace of rabbits or something on him. The local policeman Sgt Mellor kept an eye on him and us too if we were up to any mischief, scrumping apples and the like. He had a habit of cuffing us around the ear with his glove and boy did that hurt!

Brian Ransome (born 1934).

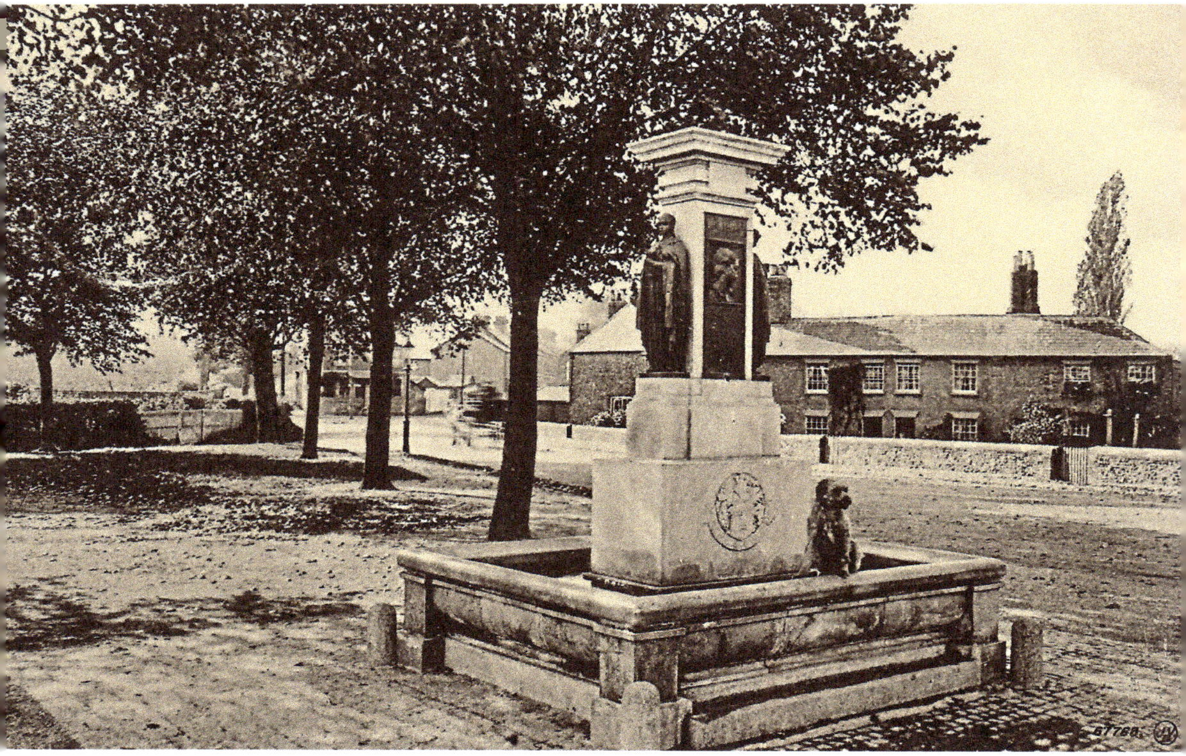

The Ouida Monument, Vinery Road.

The Lavers

I was born in my nan and grandad's house in Raingate Street; that and others were demolished to make way for the police station. Behind the house was a lane called The Lavers, which led down to meadows. I had an uncle, 'Pedlar' Palmer, who was a real Bury character. He loved the Cattle Market and kept the Rutland Arms also in Raingate Street, all the locals knew it as 'The Twizzler'. My parents lived in Westgate Road (now Out Westgate) in a long row of small cottages opposite The George pub. We moved down into Cullum Road into a cottage owned by a Mr Smith, who kept pigs near the Butts, it was a no through road then. I was around five and can remember sheltering under the table when there was an air-raid siren. Our next house was down in Vinery Road, at the bottom there was a green where the 'Ouida' memorial stood; the bus used to stop there for Hardwick Heath. There were fairs and circuses on Holywater Meadows; Mrs Davidson landlady of The George kept horses there as well. The Hardwick Fete laid on by The Round Table was also very popular. We used to catch newts down at the 'waterfall' on The Linnet at Stamford Bridge. This area around the Spread Eagle got terribly flooded in 1947, and a row of cottages at the bottom of Horringer Road got so badly damaged; they had to be demolished.

Margaret Beckwith née Johnson (born 1940).

Have you got a Light, Boy?

As a youngster, I had a great deal of affection for my grandfather, 'Tom' Allen, who enriched my life and passed down to me his sense of humour. He had a tobacconist and confectioners shop at No. 16, Guildhall Street, now part of Bedfords Estate Agents (2015). His wife, Aunt 'Dolly', received little credit though she was sharper of the two. They lived at the back of the shop separated by a glass partition that was lined with patterned wallpaper save for a tiny piece through which he and Dolly could observe people entering the shop! His customer service would never do in the twenty-first century, dispensing the wrong goods, dropping their change and teasing them. I used to deliver weekly supplies of cigarettes to various business owners in the town such as Reg Basket at Avis Electrical and George Witkowski at his hair salon in Hatter Street. Post war, Bury had several specialised tobacconists such as Sextons and Lorfords. There was also Annie Davies, a spinster who lived and worked at No. 7, Guildhall Street. She was one of life's characters, a heavy user of cosmetics, smoker and dog lover. She also liked a drink that left her temperamental and sometimes unable to sort the newspapers for the delivery rounds her shop used to provide. She treated me very well, rewarding me as I volunteered to undertake additional deliveries when others failed to turn up. I started around 6.00 a.m. in all weathers. When I was fourteen, I got an employment permit taking over a delivery round after school and on Saturday mornings from a school friend Colin Foreman. This round was for William 'Billy' Crick, a kindly man who ran a greengrocery next to Langton Garage in Hatter Street. He was very tolerant to his wife Ellie who was hard of hearing and suspect at arithmetic! Sometimes I could hardly see over the stacked groceries on the front of Billie's ancient trade bike! Such were the opportunities for young people to learn and earn.

John Saunders (born 1948).

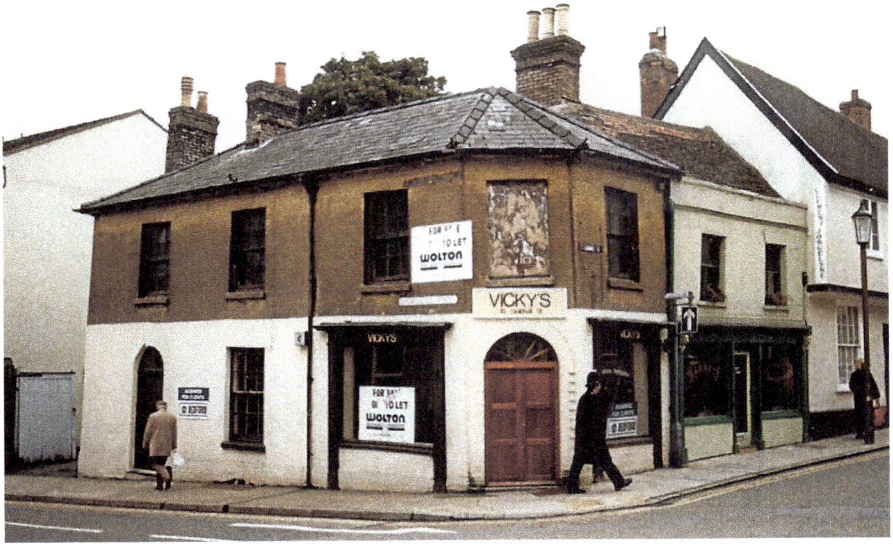

Corner of Churchgate Street and Guildhall Street, Mr Peachey had his shop here, and Tom Allen's shop was next door.

Visitors

We had a saying in our house, 'All visitors give us pleasure, some by their coming and some by their going!' We lived in an old timber-framed house in the medieval grid. It had a cellar right on the street front, the coal hole having a hinged grate in the footpath. The coalman would arrive with his open flat-bed cart and shoot 20 cwt (112 lb) sacks of coal down the chute; each one counted and sometimes weighed on the scales on the back of the cart. Although the cellar door was closed off, it created a lot of dust and work for my mother. The milkman was a daily visitor but of much more refinement. His horse and cart were always very clean with shelter for himself and his products. His horse, which I think was called Peggy, knew the daily routine by heart. She would move from stop to stop without the driver, just on his whistle. That was the norm. Fulcher's Dairy and horse stables were only 100 yards from our house, and when the drivers were around us, children could visit and feed the horses. The baker came in a horse and trap. Sometimes mother would buy at the door from his open wicker basket some extra 'bready' delights, Chelsea buns being my favourite. Often still warm with currants and mixed spices rolled inside and a sugar topping the thought of them still make my mouth water. Mr Pashler, the muffin man, was another tradesman, but without a horse. He had a trade bike with a wicker pannier on the front and would ring his bell when in the street. On opening his basket, you saw inside freshly made crumpets laying on a dazzling white cloth, what a treat for afternoon tea! One gentleman who made an occasional appearance at our door was the knife grinder with his request 'any knives or shears to sharpen'. There was rarely any business at our house as father considered it was his duty to make sure said items had an edge to them. The old boy's contraption for performing his work was a grindstone attached to the rear wheel of his bicycle. I last saw him in the late 1970s; now very old he said to me, 'I'm just a novelty these days Guv', my thanks to all of them.

Bob Charles (born 1946).

Schooldays

Taught by Norah

I was born at No. 12, Well Street, and my first school was St John's infants. On the corner with Short Brackland was my next school, the Guildhall Feoffment Girls' School. This was where Norah Robinson later to become the famous novelist, Norah Lofts, was my teacher. She lived in Northgate Street. My last school was the Silver Jubilee Girls' School, and I left there aged fifteen; the headmistress, Mrs Potter, gave me a lovely reference for work!

Gwen Brunskill née Cockle (born 1923).

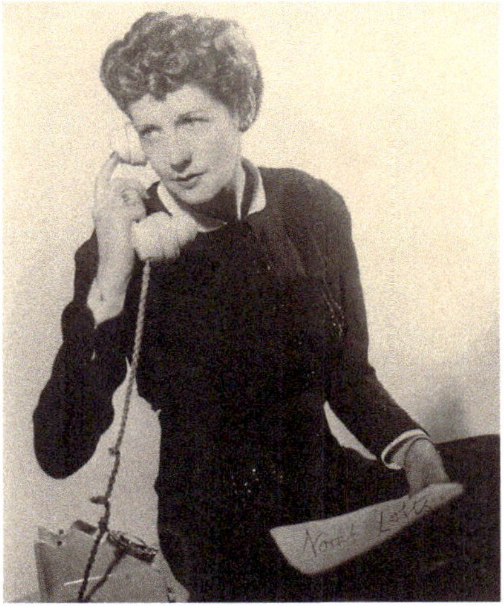

Right: Nora Robinson, also known as Norah Lofts.

Below: Gwen Brunskill (Cockle) fifth from right, back row, aged twelve in Class Three of The Guildhall Feoffment Girls' School.

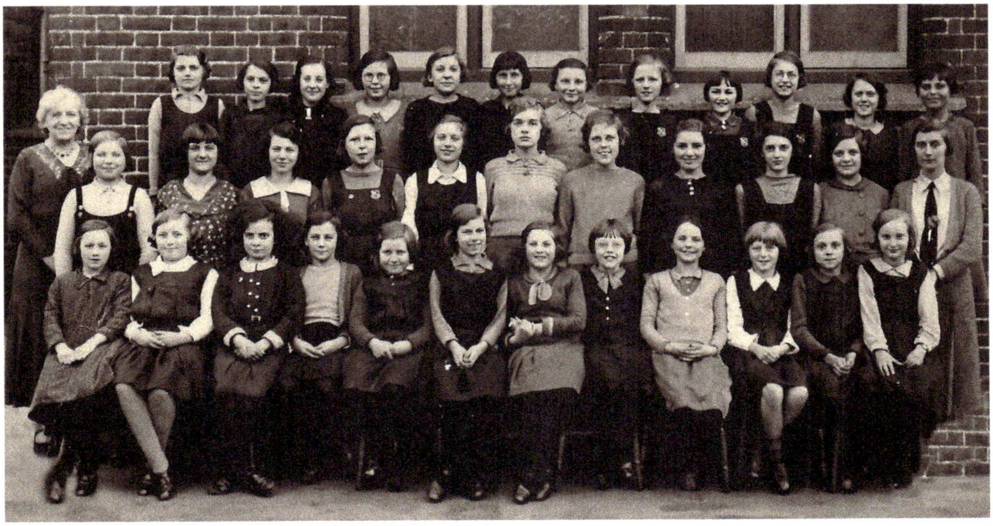

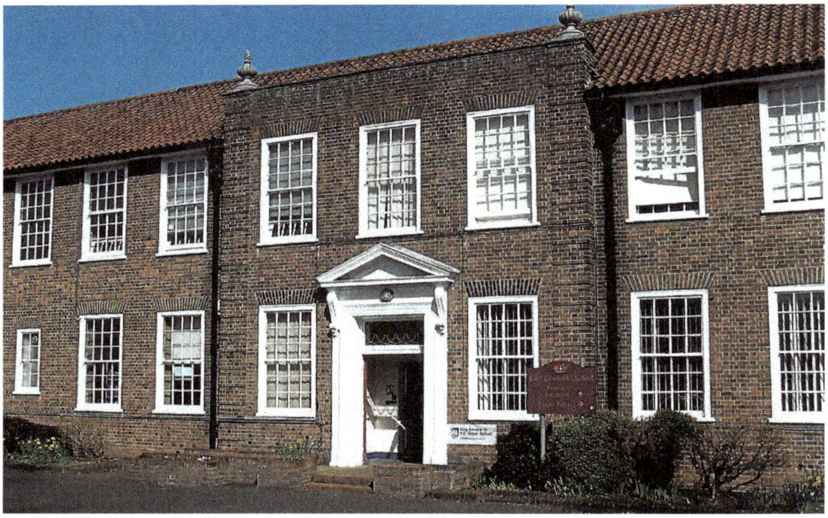

The former Jubilee School now known as KEGS, Grove Road.

Music was My Life

My first contact in coming to work in Bury at The Silver Jubilee School in 1960 was with Canon Trodden at All Saints Hall church. My wife and I lived in Wilcox Avenue. My headmaster was Mr Napier, whom I worked closely with; he even agreed to start an orchestra. By 1962, I had done *The Pirates of Penzance*, the first of several operettas at the school. The boys went on to do amazing productions of *West Side Story* and also *Oliver*. The Theatre Royal manager said could we extend our two-day slot for *Oliver* to four; we did, raising a lot of extra money. The official attendance was 102 per cent, there were people standing! I took the school orchestra down to London on that money to cut a record, a wonderful experience; this was in 1969. By joining the Operatic Society and The Irving Club in Bury, I met lots of interesting people like Ethelbert Taylor, a hairdresser, and Ron Eley, an accomplished violinist. One day, a pupil said, 'Sir, I'm in the Scouts and we're putting on a gang show and we need a pianist', I asked my wife if this was okay, and she said, 'Roland, our son wants to join the cubs but they are full, if he can get in, you can play the piano'. He became a cub! I ended up producing at least seven productions at the Theatre Royal for the Bury Mayor's own Scout troop. My wife once got my children together and said, 'This is your father' as I was spending so much time away from them. Of course she was right. I went on to have a wonderful twenty-three years at Westley Middle School retiring at sixty-five, there was so much going on there too, and it was unbelievable. Somebody once said to me that Bury St Edmunds is like a big village, everyone knew everybody else, I couldn't argue with that. After many years, I still have contact with some former pupils, many who have achieved success in the music world. Perhaps the pinnacle of my career if you could describe it as such was getting 750 pupils singing in unison, Jerusalem with an orchestra, a truly fantastic moment. The journey through my school life has meant meeting so many amazing people.

Lawford Smith (born 1929).

Stone Picking

When I was at the Jubilee, a new playing field had just been laid and the stones kept working their way to the top. Me and a friend, John Turner, were given the job of picking them up and putting them into a wheelbarrow. We soon got bored with this and started mucking about pushing each other in the barrow. The PE teacher Jeff Holder caught us doing this and gave us both a bloody good hiding.

Keith Mothersole (born 1946).

Home Comforts

As soon as I was old enough, I went to the kindergarten that Miss David ran at the Manor House on Honey Hill. When her five-year lease expired, she moved up to Moreton Hall which saved everyone a lot of money as it had the same initials, MH! After a prep school at Southwold, I went to Uppingham School where I did articles for the family law firm. This involved courses for five years including two stints in London and sitting exams. It was a pleasure to come home to enjoy home comforts and treats which in those days were rare and highly prized. I qualified in 1965 and went to Lowestoft as an assistant solicitor to gain experience outside Bury St Edmunds.

Ted Ashton (born 1941).

Crossing the river

I was one of eight children, and we lived in Tollgate Lane. Then, the lane finished near to where Philip Road is today and was very handy for my father James Sansom to get to work as he was a guard on the railways. We all had to walk to the nearest school that was in Fornham St Martin. There was just one big classroom for all the boys and girls to use; their ages ran from five to eleven. When the River Lark used to flood down by the Tollgate, the only way us kids living the wrong side of it to get to school was to be ferried over by boat!

Marjorie Frost née Sansom (born 1912).

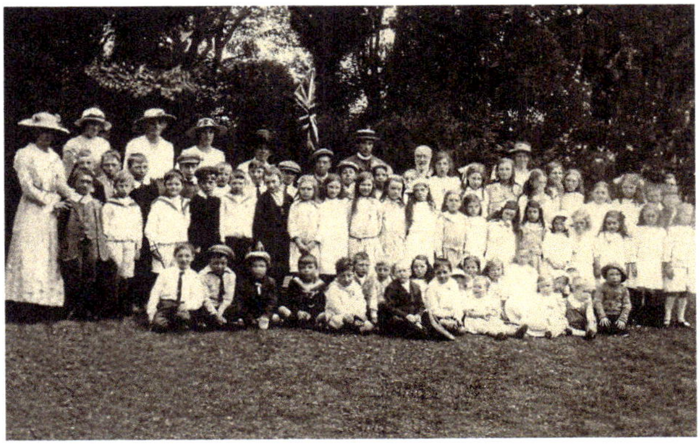

Marjorie Frost (Sansom) sixth from the right, second row, Fornham St Martin School, *c.* 1922.

Call Me Sir

My father was a professional footballer for Norwich City and at the end of his career came to Bury Town as player/coach. Through his connections, several ex-Norwich players formed the backbone of the town's great early 1960s side. I attended the King Edward VI Grammar school; then, it was a boarding school with many of the boarders, the sons of service personnel. Going to school on a Saturday was a new experience for me; the morning spent in lessons, and the afternoon, compulsory sports. Those not sporty enough participated in the CCF, the Combined Cadet Force. I enjoyed the school, discipline was firm, and if a master walked into the classroom you all stood up – you could hear a pin-drop. There was only one female teacher then, Kate Kilpatrick, who taught biology and always insisted on being addressed as sir! I was lucky enough to be selected for West Suffolk boys football team, something the Grammar School never really got involved with. On occasions, I even played for Bury Reserves who played at night under floodlights. The head called me in one day to speak to me about this and reminded me I was down to play for the school in the afternoon, he said this came first so I ended up playing one game after the other!

Bobby Flack (born 1943).

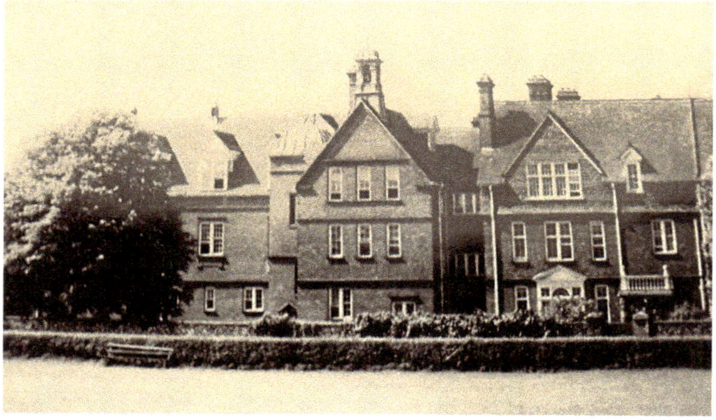

King Edward VI Grammar School.

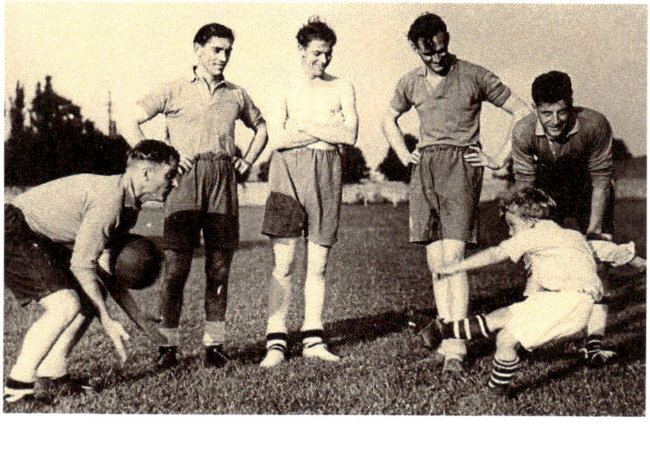

A young Bobby Flack with Bury Town footballers in 1948.

Back to School

When I was little, I went to Miss Miller's Nursery School opposite the cathedral on Angel Hill, followed by the East Anglian Prep School that catered for six- to eight-year-old children. After that, I was supposed to sit the Culford School entrance exam. My father, Maurice Wilson who had Eastgate Street Post Office, was very strict and insisted I took the exam. I didn't want to go there, and on the Friday night before the exam, I feigned appendicitis. I missed the exam, recovering miraculously by the Saturday evening! I thought that was the end of it, all but six months later, I was taken to Culford School by my father with threats ringing in my ears from my grandfather that if I didn't sit the exam, he would send me away to boarding school! I remember sitting in this Dickensian classroom with a teacher dressed in a long gown and a mortar board on his head! I managed to put my name at the top of the page but never answered a single question. Two weeks later, my father had a meeting with Dr Storey, the Culford Headmaster who said, 'Well Mr Wilson it doesn't look like your son wants to come to Culford after all; he never answered a single question'. My backside is still stinging fifty years on! Anyway I never went to boarding school and ended up going to St Edmundsbury School and then the Silver Jubilee. I left there at seventeen with three O-levels to work at Fair Tax Travel. I didn't like it there, I was not alone! I asked father if I could go back to school to get further qualifications, to which he agreed providing I knuckled down. I went and saw Mr Byers, the careers master, who reluctantly agreed as I had not been away from school that long. However, I was somewhat embarrassed when I had to sit my six-month-long course alongside a giggling class of schoolgirls at the adjacent Jubilee Girls' School! Fortunately, a boy, John Fisk eventually joined me. I ended up getting sufficient qualifications to get a job with the Sun Alliance Assurance Company.

Grenville Wilson (born 1949).

Portland School

I went to Portland House School in Guildhall Street run by two sisters, the Misses Underwoods. During the war when the sirens sounded the warning, we would go into the cellars, coming up on the all clear. I'm sure a siren used to sound during the 1950s on the Playfields in Kings Road to alert firemen. I went to Miss David's Manor House School via Church Walks; that was an experience to be had. I used to be envious of all the children playing games there like hopscotch. It seemed to me Bury was teeming with life, each area of the town having its own self-supporting community. I used to go about with my parents a lot even helping at their laundry, ironing hankies!

Sheila Bayne née Forbes (born 1938).

Sports Field and J. T. Field

In 1953, I moved to York Road from Horringer and then to Stanton in 1959. The transition of moving schools was quite traumatic, as when I started at the County Grammar on our return to Bury. I didn't like school much and even less the sports lessons on the playing fields up at Beetons Way. We had a two-lesson slot to get there and back for the next, this included changing! 1964 saw the last year the school was in Northgate Street before its move up to Beetons Way as County Upper. I can remember helping to move all the library books up there! I had a Saturday job at J. T. Field in Abbeygate Street; my older sister Doreen worked there full-time. It was an exclusive ladies wear shop; I got £1 a day, but a friend of mine who worked at 'Woolies' only got 10*s*.

Liz Fayers née Ward (born 1948).

Moving Around

My Welsh father was in the army and met my mother who was working in a munitions factory. After the war, dad got a job working for Fulcher Farms in and around Bury. Our first tied cottage was at North Hill, Rushbrook. Mother used to walk me to the little school at Nowton; it had a large open fire surrounded by a fireguard in the one big schoolroom. Imagine that being allowed today? We then lived at Horsecroft Farm before settling down at what is today's Dairy Cottage in Home Farm Lane; it was two thatched cottages then. I went to the Feoffment though can't remember much about it except having to learn a song for the coronation. I then went to the Jubilee. I worked at Woolworths on Saturdays and during holidays for two years mainly on the sweet counter with pick'n'mix, hot peanuts and cashews lovely. I suppose if 'Woolies' had allowed us to stuff ourselves silly in the first few days, we wouldn't have been tempted! At the Jubilee, I stayed on to do a commercial course; there was also a nursing course you could go on, even girls from the grammar school went on them. Perhaps one of my strongest memories was the head, Mrs Crocker. She had a presence about her and could walk into a noisy room and you could suddenly hear a pin-drop!

Beris Culyer née Walton (born 1944).

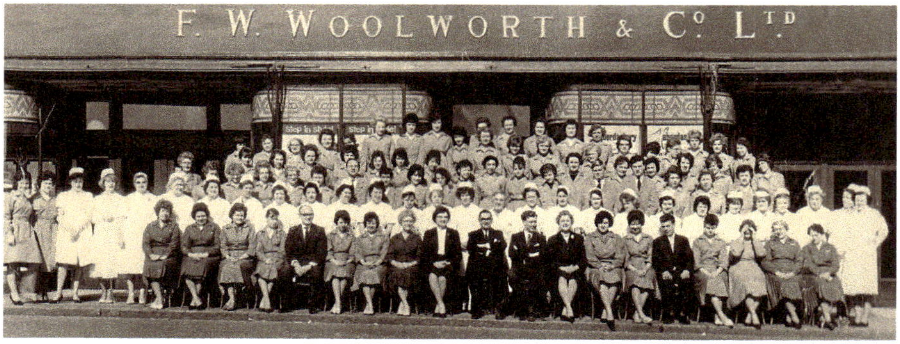

Woolworths Staff around 1960.

First Prize

I loved school and while young followed the older children to the Tollgate School near to where I lived. When I eventually went to school, I developed yellow jaundice, being ill for quite a while. I enjoyed sports so hated being in bed. I liked visiting my grandparents down at the Spread Eagle; Grandad sold his flowers and veg outside his cottage, and on occasions, Eldon Griffiths bought some when he passed by. My gran never knew that grandad grew strawberries as he always sold them before she had a chance to see them! When I was around eight, gran took me into Mr Peachey's second-hand shop, she loved going in there, but I was embarrassed in case any of my friends saw me. I played on swings in Severn Road separated from fields by a fence; sometimes the farmer threatened to shoot us with his gun if we climbed over it. Of course, he never did, but it was a good deterrent. As kids, we picked peas at Laflins Farm getting a big bag for a few bob, and I can remember walking to Westley fruit Farm and picking fruit there. I never had a bike so it was a bit of a trudge. At the Jubilee, I once went on a school trip, and as a school leaver, I had to write an essay about my experience. My teacher was really surprised when I won first prize for it in a competition. Strangely the book that I wrote it in disappeared for a while, but it turned out one of the school governors had taken it home to read as he enjoyed it so much; I still have that book somewhere.

Anne Vickers née Williams (born 1950).

Elocution

When I was around thirteen, I represented the Silver Jubilee at a public speaking competition held in Colchester. One of my teachers had given me elocution lessons in her spare time. I had to remember an extract from *The Lion, the Witch and the Wardrobe*. I was up against several other schools, and I spoke on what seemed an enormous stage in front of loads of people, coming second. I still have that certificate.

Lorna Allen née Taylor (born 1946).

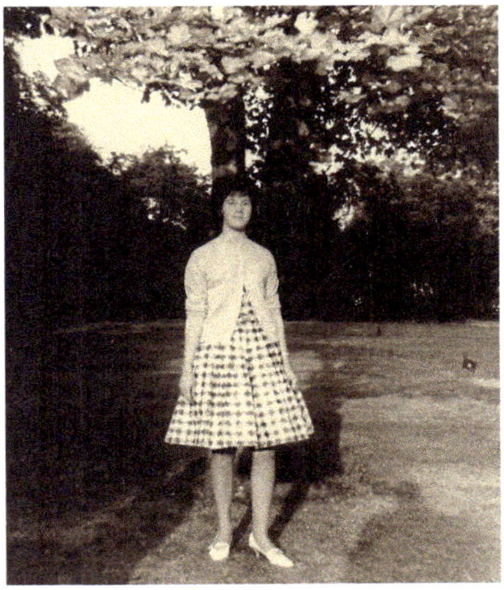

Lorna Allen (Taylor) aged fifteen in the Abbey Gardens.

Slow Races and Writing

We lived in Chalk Road; dad was a boiler man at the old West Suffolk Hospital. Mum was a hard worker; she did the laundry for Bury Town Football Club (FC) and had a couple of cleaning jobs, one at Victoria Infants' School which I went to. I can remember having snail races there and the winner etching their name into the wall. At the Silver Jubilee, I was deputy Head Boy and in Stanley House. The other three school houses were Hadow, Fisher and Forster. I won a wooden shield for composing an essay on a futuristic Bury; it took me ages to write as I wasn't the quickest of writers. I wonder how much of that essay came true. After school, I worked in the stock room of Walkers Stores and also did a paper round for Saunders in King's Road. Frewers, the Bakers, was also in King's Road next to Bury Town's ground, and they did a roaring trade in filled rolls when a match was on!

Bernard Taylor (born 1939).

Mascot

We still had blackboards and chalk at St Peter's school when I went there. The toilets were outside, and you were given four sheets of paper to use! I was probably at the Guildhall Feoffment when I was made mascot for Bury Town FC. Mind you having your grandfather as the treasurer and father as the secretary certainly helped! After the referee tossed up his half-crown at the beginning of the game, I was given it. I did quite well out of that for around three seasons though I'm not sure if dad had something to do with it. I went to the Jubilee, and I played a lot of tennis there even playing in a big tournament run by Nestles; I suppose I wasn't that bad a player. The boys' and girls' playground was separated by a line down the middle; you were in BIG trouble if you crossed that line.

Peter Pettit (born 1955).

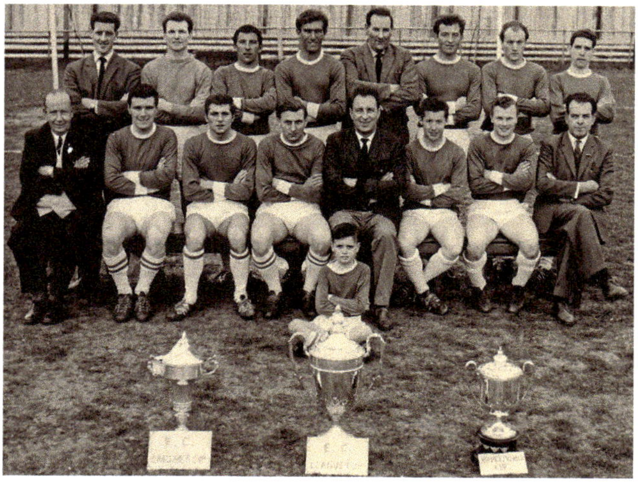

Bury Town FC, winners of the Eastern Counties League and Cup and Suffolk Premier Cup 1963–64 with mascot Peter Pettit.

School Heroes

My mother's maiden name was Alice Mary Taylor, but everyone called her 'Doll' as she was so short. I lived with her and her parents at No. 52, Northgate Street, her father's house. My childhood was easy and uncomplicated. Like lots of other boys in the town where you lived decided the gang you were in. My first school was St John's Infants. One day I was with my cousin Ted in the playground when teacher Miss Candler called the children in. She did this by clapping her hands loudly, the trouble was we never heard her, resulting in us getting into the classroom late plus six swipes of her ruler across the palms of our hands. We never cried which went down well with our classmates, but we never let on it really did hurt! My next school was The Guildhall Feoffment. One day I wore my 'Sunday best' patent leather shoes there; I scuffed one, splitting the toe. The poor teacher was worried that mother would come up to the school and blame them for allowing these expensive shoes to get damaged. She never did.

Peter Dove (born 1927).

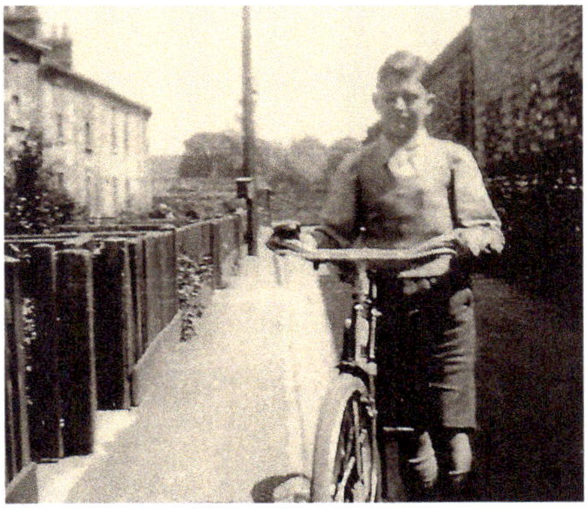

Peter Dove at Reeds Buildings.

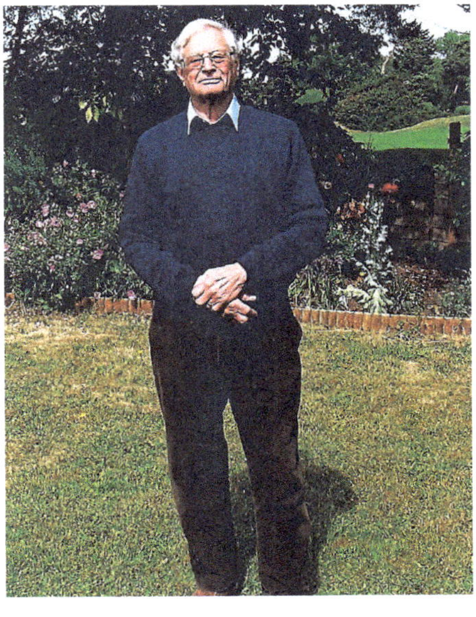

Peter Dove in 2015.

The Misses Smith

As a young boy, I went to a school at 1, Out Risbygate, run by Florrie, Nellie and Gurtie Smith, all sisters. They always dressed fashionably with somewhat rouged cheeks. I walked there from my home at No. 36, full of trepidation and thoughts of getting picked on by Priors lads as I was only small; I never was. Every mid-morning Miss Nellie would appear with a tray of odd cups with milk in for us ten children that sat around a big table. We were given a set of dominoes to play with, but nobody had a clue how to play the game as the rules weren't provided! We didn't play outside, but the toilet we used was at the bottom of the garden. I went onto St Edmundsbury, getting terrible confused which class I was in because of the large number of children there. I then had a year at the Jubilee that I enjoyed before going onto Culford. I disliked Latin and managed to get it changed over to woodwork, which I loved doing though I never told father. He promised me if I gained my school certificate, he would buy me a motor bike; I passed but didn't get the bike, instead a car a year later!

Anthony Childs (born 1932).

A Bright Spark

During the Second World War, my father, an agricultural contractor, met my mother who was in the land army. They acquired Gaol Farm in Sicklesmere Road where I was born. I was around five or six when I went down to the yard where I had made myself a den. I lit a match but dropped it on my trousers which were oily from playing among the plant and machinery. I was set alight and ended up being rushed to Norwich hospital where skin grafts were taken from my mother to put on my burnt legs, I still have the scars today! When I was older, I thought I might pass the eleven plus and go to Culford School, but I failed and ended up going to the Silver Jubilee. The only thing I liked about that place was sports. Around a week before, I was due to leave me and some of my school mates removed the door handles from all the doors of the prefab block, boy was there trouble over that. We thought we got away with it, but we were found out and were made an example of when we got the cane off Mr Butler on the school stage at assembly in front of the whole school!

Harry Sturgeon (born 1951).

Snoozing in School

My grandmother lived in York Road, and when mum separated from dad, we went to live with her; I was around five at that time. Mr Lambert used to run a grocery store in York Road, and we used our ration books there. We then moved into Queens Road; we had gas mantles for lights. I went to the Victoria Street Infants School and can recall having a nap in the afternoon as the teachers couldn't be sure that we might be woken up during the night because of the war. In the terrible winter of 1947, the snow was so deep; it was nearly up to the tops of your legs! We had to thaw the top part of our bottles of school milk around the 'bogey' stove so we could drink it.

Shirley Pattle née Wraight (born 1940).

Accountable

Born and brought up on the Mildenhall Estate, my first school was Tollgate School, and it was both primary and junior school. I went to the Jubilee Boys' School when I was eleven. Our year was one of the biggest intakes ever with six classes, most were with forty boys in. Some of the teachers there used to hand out punishment piecemeal. I left there and went to work for T. H. Nice as a trainee accountant and then moved onto Burrells, the sister company in Cotton Lane. They in turn were taken over by Cowies, and I ended my working life as general manager running all of their three branches.

John Brunskill (born 1950).

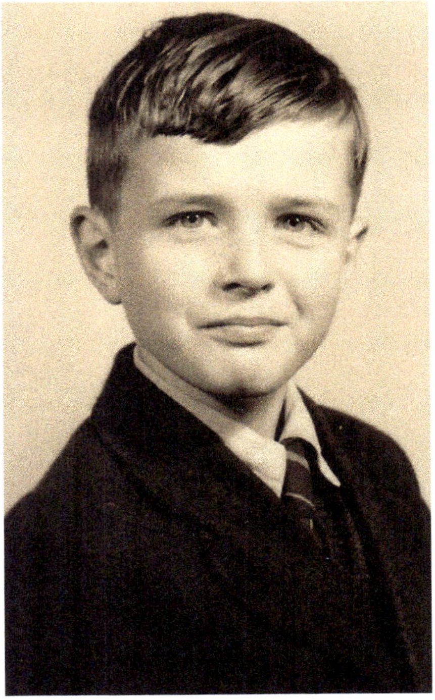

John Brunskill aged twelve.

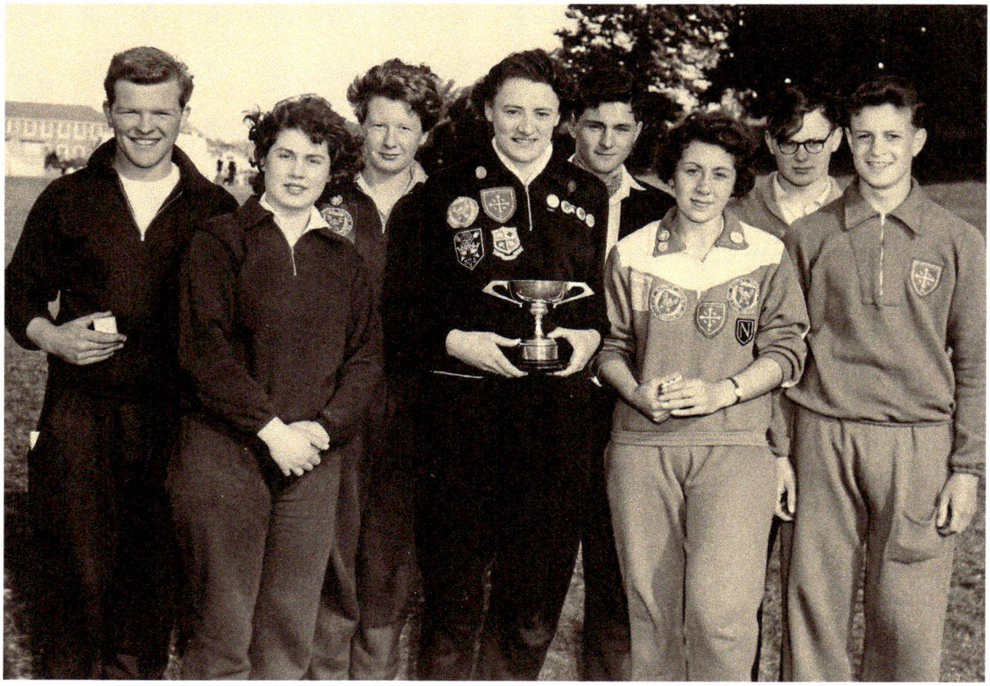

Olive Catton, centre, with other successful athletes.

Pretty Quick

My mum Lily was a cook and domestic to the Dearbergh family of Thurston. My father Albert Catton was chauffeur to Dr Cockram; we lived at No. 17a, Northgate Street next door to the doctor at No. 17. Dad was also a Sunday school superintendent and elder at West Road Hall; my Christian upbringing has been the mainstay of my life. My friends went to the County Grammar School, but I went to the Jubilee where I went on to become head girl following in my sister Mary's footsteps. I excelled at sports; my school report said if Olive spent more time in the classroom than on the sports field, she would be more academically successful. I was the youngest competitor to go to the All England Schools Championships representing West Suffolk. The school had to borrow some men's spikes for me! I completed a secretarial course and left to join the Bury Free Press as secretary to manager Mr Thompson and then the editor Mr Appel. I had thought about joining the police but couldn't because in those days women could only join at twenty years old. I had an interview with Mr Ridd, the then Chief Constable, who said he would take me on and he did a day after I turned twenty. He was a nice man but did have an affliction, a twitch in his eye! I had joined West Suffolk Athletics Club and held several records; in fact, when I was in the police, I won the national 100 yards title for West Suffolk Constabulary. There was a headline in the Bury Free Press 'The fastest police woman in the country!' I also played for Bury Women's Hockey and Netball teams.

Olive Catton (born 1938).

Working Life

Getting Wet

As I walked to work at the Sun Alliance offices in Abbeygate Street one Monday in September 1968, I noticed water bubbling out of a drain. It had been raining heavily so I thought nothing of it. At around 10 a.m., my father rang to ask if I could go home as his post office was now flooded! One of the staff, Gordon Warren, offered me some of his son's old clothes to put on, the trouble was his son was over 6-feet tall, and the clothes drowned me, 'scuse the pun'. I took off my work suit and climbed into them. Gordon took me by car to Mustow Street, but it was clearly impossible to get across Eastgate Bridge as the water was too high. Turning the car around, he drove up to Southgate Green where people were being ferried across the river by a tractor and trailer. I made my way to Eastgate Street and went down the side of The Ram pub to the rear of the post office. Wading through chest-high water, I eventually managed to get up on the flat roof extension. My father had been incredibly busy getting all the stock up higher than the water. All he lost was one chocolate bar!

Grenville Wilson (born 1949).

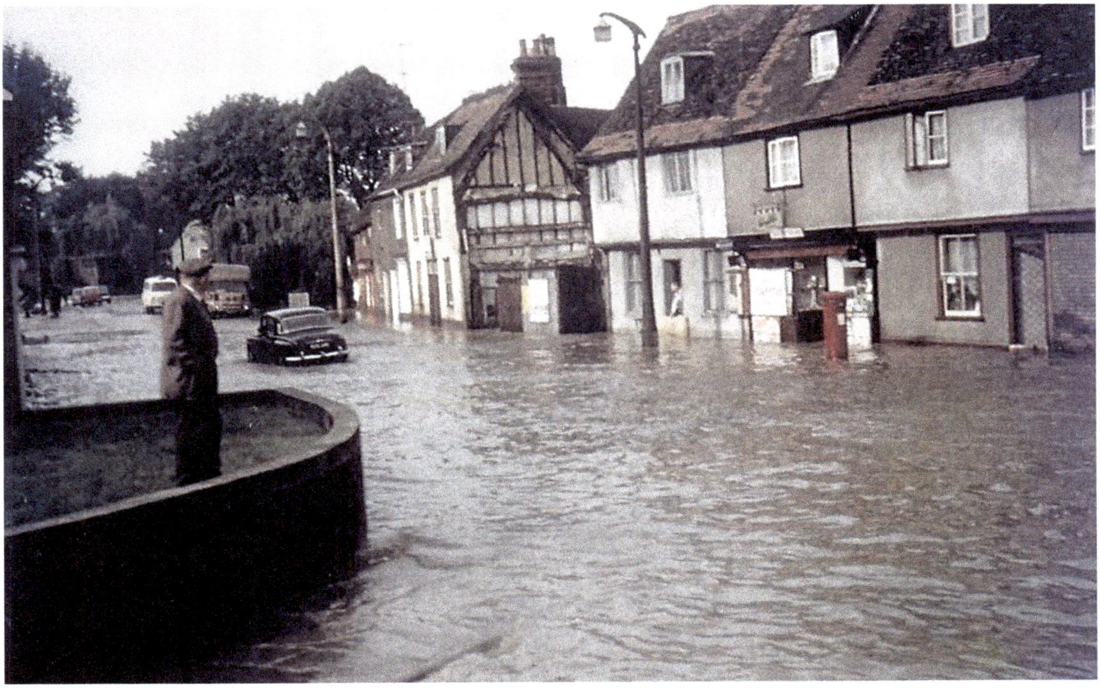

Eastgate Street and the flooding of 1968.

Milkman

My grandfather and father used to run a laundry in Horringer Road; I would help my mother put the sheets through the rollers. I went to Pawseys as an apprentice compositor but left after three years. I did a couple of jobs before a neighbour said why not be a milkman like him. I was married and then living in Winthrop Road. I enjoyed the fresh air and finishing early meant I could help my wife with the foster care she gave children. One of my mates, Barry Hatcher, had a father who was a milkman with a horse and cart. He used to deliver to old Mrs Booty who always gave his horse an apple. One day she forgot, and the horse nearly wrecked the shop front trying to get in for its treat! When St Edmunds Dairy sold out to Dairy Crest, I became a lorry driver for Jewsons for twelve years.

Keith Mothersole (born 1946).

Over Qualified

After Bury Grammar school, I went to Newcastle-upon-Tyne University and graduated in 1969. I started applying for various jobs throughout the country. One interview I went for was in Wakefield at the council there. The interviewer said at the start, 'I don't really agree with graduate trainees, I was brought up the hard way'. You could say I wasn't surprised when I wasn't offered the job. I came back to Bury, and my dad saw an advert in the Bury Free Press for a junior clerk with possible computer training at the council. I applied for it and got it though I was overqualified. I was a general 'dogsbody' at first doing everything and anything including collecting pennies from the ladies toilets in The Traverse! On occasions, a colleague and I used to go to Lloyds Bank in the Buttermarket to collect the wages for the council workers. We tried to act nonchalant; however, I'm not sure if we didn't draw more attention to ourselves! Sometimes I was relief cashier at the front desk in the Borough Offices on Angel Hill. Other times I was at the Corporation yard in Kings Road where 'Nobby' Nobbs, the town foreman, read out the workers names, and I would hand them their pay packet and collect a signature. These were all the sort of jobs you did to get on in life.

David Addy (born 1948).

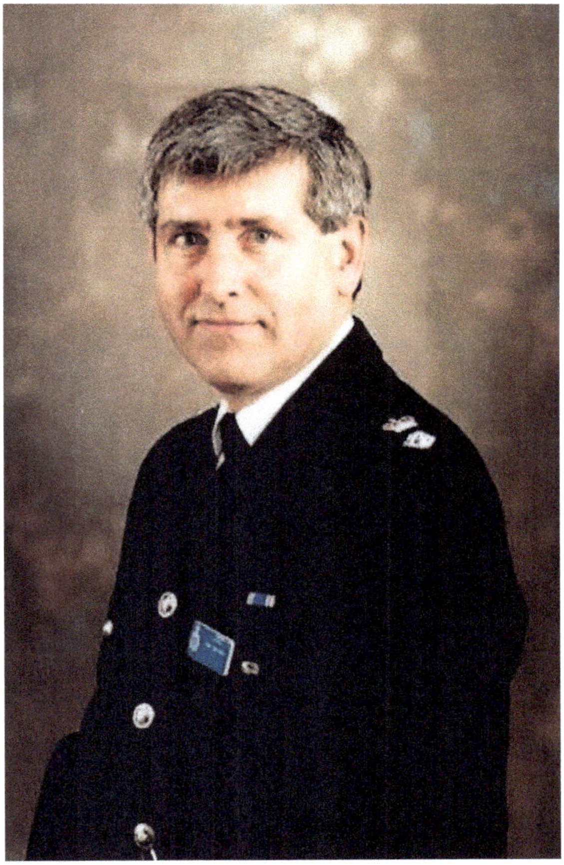

Chief Superintendent John Saunders in 1990.

Low Crime

My career of thirty-two years in policing followed my father who was an inspector in Bury. From 1982 to 1986, I was in charge of the area's detectives and subsequently the town's superintendent. Crime in the Bury area was relatively low, and it was considered one of the safest towns in the country. Despite this, people had their concerns about badly parked vehicles, speeding and noisy children at bus shelters! This meant keeping good public and business relationships. One of my successes was appointing Tony Gardiner as the town centre constable; conspicuous by his beard and air of authority, he was highly respected and effective. I made a real effort to get to know Bury's residents. Civic functions and public events consumed a lot of time, but interacting with people was essential in getting their support. In those days, I was sufficiently important to walk at the head of the carnival floats! However, it was not all peace and quiet because on 5 July 1986, public disorder happened. A political march turned ugly with clashes of opposing factions, and missiles were thrown resulting in the first sight of police in riot gear being deployed in the town, but it is the good times and the good people of Bury that I remember in my stint at Bury.

John Saunders (born 1948).

Waiting for the Call

On leaving school, I worked as a home help for Dr Stork, who lived at No. 3, Looms Lane. It wasn't very well paid because I was young. I didn't stay there long as I was waiting to start as a telephonist at the telephone exchange in Whiting Street. When my chance came, I had to go for an eyesight test to see whether I was colour-blind for the different wires and to check on my height. I had to be at least 5 feet 4 inches as the connecting plugs were up high. For two years, I was on probation and during this time went to evening classes to do Maths and English. When the probation had finished, I went to Slough on a final six-week training course, I was sixteen then. On my return to Bury, I had to sit a Civil Service Examination, this was in the Constitutional Club; I sat it all on my own! Finally, after I had signed the Official Secrets Act, I could call myself a telephonist. I worked as one for seven years during the day and nine years in the evening after I got married. I ended my working life as a receptionist at Bloomfield House Clinic in Looms Lane.

Daphne Elliston née Warren (born 1932).

Gullible

I always wanted to be a hairdresser, and while at school, I got a Saturday job at Fulcher & King in The Traverse. While here I was sent out on a fool's errand one day to get some striped paint for a barber's pole, after all what did I know? I did my apprenticeship at Dennis Burgess hair salon in Risbygate Street. My first day was eventful. The water heater had packed up, and I was told to get a pail of water from downstairs as the salon was on the first floor. I got to the top and dropped it right down the stairs! I worked for Dennis for twenty years before leaving and running my own business in the Regency Hotel.

Rosemary Rayson née Vickers (born 1948).

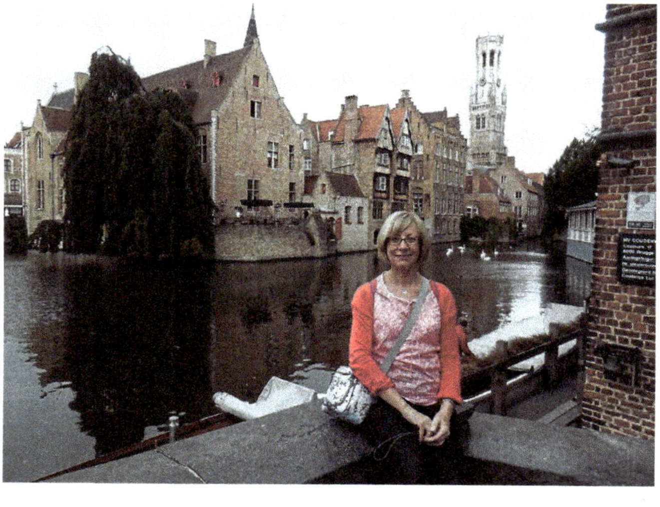

Rosemary Rayson on holiday in Bruges.

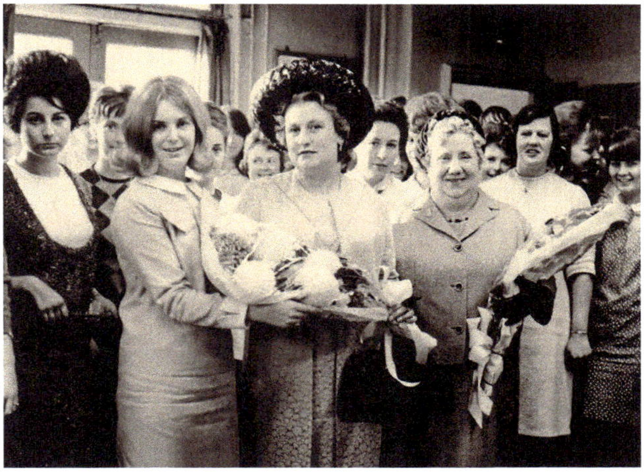

Wendy Wells on left with the Mayoress, Mrs Steel, during her visit to the Telephone Exchange 1965.

Self-improvement

I couldn't get on with some of the teachers at the Jubilee and left without any certificates. I had an interview for a job as a telephonist at the telephone exchange; I was up against girls from the grammar school. Surprisingly, I got the job and went on a six-week course down at Canterbury; this was the first time I had travelled by train. The exchange was manual then and required a lot of staff; over 120 people mainly women worked shifts there. The supervisor was a Dorothy Dixon, and she was ever so strict! I worked there for eight years from 1960 and even became the union representative; perhaps I wasn't as thick as I thought. I then went abroad returning in 1973 to work as the secretary to the manager of Motor Body Specialist in Eastgate Street. I left here after a while and embarked on a new career, gaining qualifications to work in the Adult Training Centre in Hollow Road. This eventually led me to working within social services until I retired as Locality Resource Manager in 2005.

Wendy Wells née Smith (born 1945).

Good Craftsmen

I started my working life at sixteen as an apprentice carpenter for Direct Labour of Bury St Edmunds Borough Council working on the new council estates being built around Bury. Their clerk of works was a church going, non-swearing perfectionist, Ernie Bunkle. For example, all the screw head slots had to line up on door hinges, woe betide you if you tried to put one over him. However, if you had a problem, he would help you sort it out. One day some plasterer's walls didn't meet Ernie's standards so he just drew crosses over them and told them to chip the plaster off and redo! After five years for the council, I had a spell with Barbrookes. My brother Brian had worked for W. J. Bakers and left them to start up his own business, Kemp Builders. I joined him after a while and worked with him for the rest of my working life, always producing good work.

Malcolm Ransome (born 1941).

Nice Work

My first job was secretary to Mr Stutely, the parts manager at T H Nice & Co. At Christmas time, the Thetford, Ely and two Bury branches all sat down for a slap-up meal at The Angel Hotel. I left Nice's in 1963 to marry Malcolm, my husband, and then worked for Hunters & Olivers wine merchants in Abbeygate Street. Nobody liked going into their cellars because of the haunted tunnels that were supposed to be down there! Before we were married, we liked to go to the Athenaeum for the dances, I liked to wear a full-skirted taffeta dress, which were all the rage then for ballroom dancing. Unfortunately, when the Teddy Boys moved in, we moved out!

Shirley Ransome née Pike (born 1942).

Greasy Fingers

Straight from school, I went to work at Mann Egertons in Fornham Road. Like all youngsters, I smoked cigarettes. One day one of the workers there, Edgar Grainger, came up to me and said, 'Boy, never smoke ciggies cos of your greasy fingers, smoke a pipe'. So I followed his advice and filled two pipes first thing in the morning sitting down at docky time with him while he puffed away on his and I mine! I enlisted in the Grenadier Guards in 1957 and was in Cyprus for around fourteen months. After three years in the Guards, I married my wife Pauline, and the old Guards network helped me to get a job as a chauffeur/valet for Lord De Ramsey at Abbots Ripton. It was amazing driving his Aston Martin DB4 and his Ferrari. We returned to Bury, and I got a job as a caretaker for the Borough Council. I was custodian for some lovely buildings in the town such as The Manor House, ghosts and all! I later moved to Suffolk County Council, living in an old cottage in the Great Churchyard. After I was made redundant, I finished my working life at Scotts the opticians, and I still enjoy a pipe.

Bernard Taylor (born 1939).

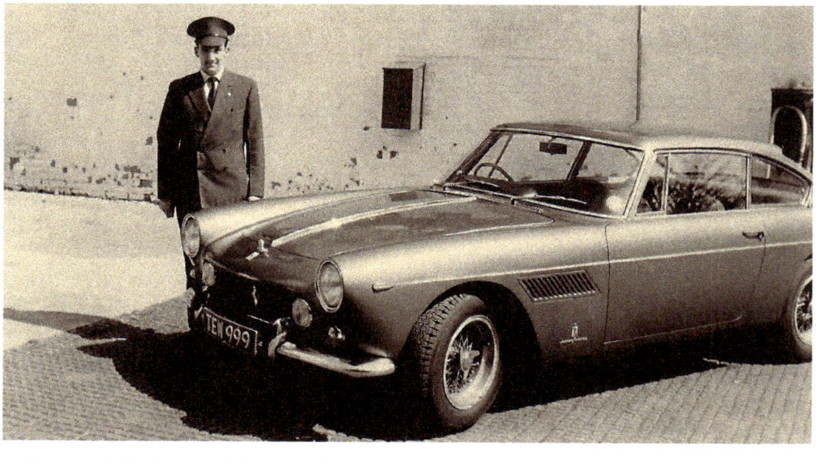

Chauffeur Bernard Taylor with his employer's Aston Martin DB4.

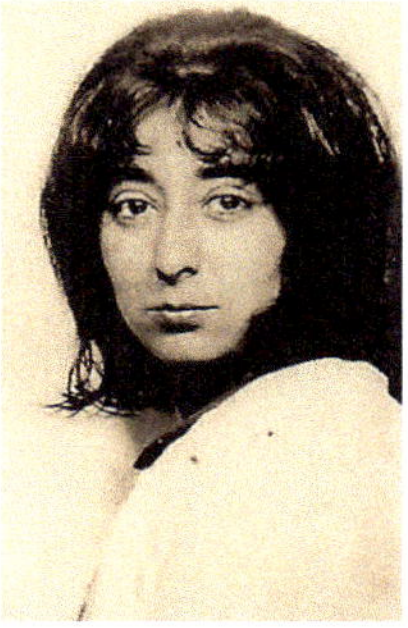

Carol Waters aged 18.

Different Managers

On leaving school I got a job as an usherette at The Odeon for three years. One night this Italian fella wouldn't take no for an answer so I slapped him round the face. Unfortunately for me the manager Mr Kyle came by as it happened and sacked me on the spot! After a couple of odd jobs, I went to work for Douglas Warnes clothing factory, the manager Peter Smith was a lovely person to work for.

Carol Waters (born 1945).

Still There

I remember when the Corn Exchange was split forming shops below the large hall so a large temporary wooden building, known as the Market Hall, was built at the end of Prospect Row. It was in use long after the work on the Corn Exchange had finished, especially for bingo. Nearby on the playfields, the Water Board had a pumping station, the Council a tarmac dump and Eastern Electricity (EE) a depot. After doing three years vehicle maintenance for the Co-op, in around 1967, I started working for the EE Board as it was then known. I am coming up to having done forty-eight years and look forward to retirement at the end of 2015.

Reg Cowlin (born 1948).

London and North Eastern Railway

It was common in my day to go to work where your father did; you accepted it as the norm. So when I left school, I went to work for the London and North Eastern Railway just before it became British Railway Eastern Region in 1948. My job was in the Bury yard signal box. However, after I did National Service I came back to Bury and took a sideways move and worked into the booking office. When the Beeching cuts came though I decided my working life was to be elsewhere so I went to W Vintens in Western Way in the accounts department. I left after seven years, moving on to work in accounts for Baker Builders till I retired.

David Ridgeon (born 1932).

Guinness Men

On leaving school I worked at Barclays Bank until 1967. My dad, John Ward was war-disabled and was advised to give up his job on the land by his doctors. He had worked part time for Mrs Oliver in Westgate Street and one day she said to him 'well John, looks like you will have to get yourself a pub, leave it with me'. In a short time he started his new career as a publican, ten years at The Old Angel till it closed, and then eleven years at the Rose & Crown. I worked shifts sometimes; you could say I did my apprenticeship then as did my husband Tony. Dad retired on his 65th birthday in 1986 and we took over the Rose & Crown, we still have it. Over the years we have been aware of the ghosts there though never actually seeing one but always mindful of their presence, the odd thing being moved or a casual glance of 'what was that'. Of the many tales associated with the pub was when dad was still licensee and the Brewery Bond in Maynewater Lane was being built, there were six Irishmen living on site. Every working day without fail one of them would come in and pre-order twelve Guinness for their morning and lunchtime breaks and at knocking off. If that was not enough, after a spruce up and their evening meal they would return and have another five or six pints each, they were never any trouble at all!

Liz Fayers née Ward (born 1948).

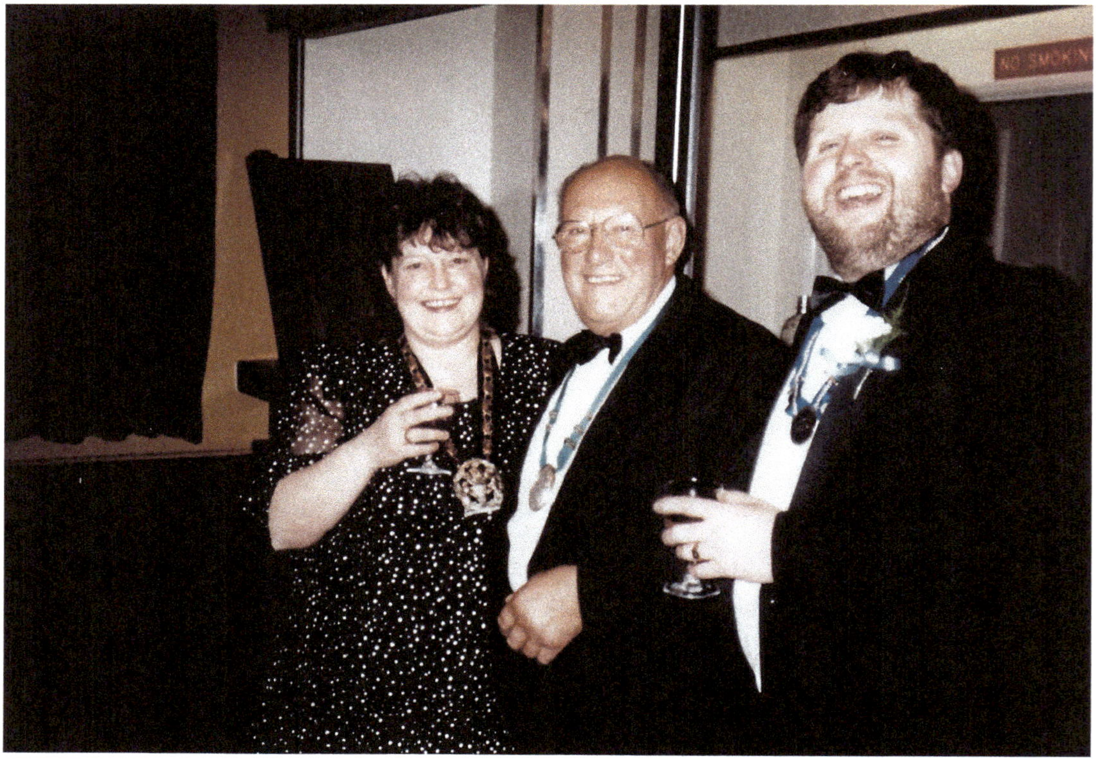

Liz and Tony Fayers with John Ward (centre) wearing their Chains of Office within The Licensed Victuallers Association.

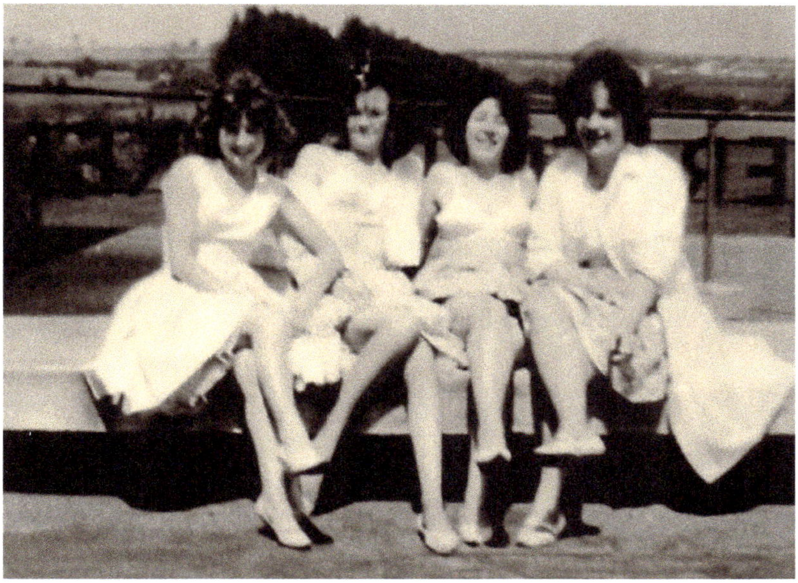

Pamela Cannell on the right with friends sunning themselves on the Co-op Bakery roof.

Flour and Flowers

I left the Jubilee to work at the Co-op Bakery in Western Way. It was a hard job working as I did in the flour room, which was high up in the bakery, but the smell of the baking bread was lovely. The hours were long and I worked there for six and half years. Out of my 30*s* a week pay packet my mum took 10*s* for my keep. She said she didn't really need it but it would teach me the value of money. As an only child when I got married she gave me all those ten bobs back as she had saved them up towards my wedding costs!

Pamela Cannell née Baker (born1945).

Very Strict

I remember Mrs Leggett, who was a PE teacher at the Jubilee, she also took us for needlework, which I loved. There was also a maths teacher there called Miss Strickland, strict by name and strict by nature! I left school at fifteen and went to Harveys clothing factory in Tayfen Road. I didn't like it much as their big glass roof made working inside the factory very hot, I left soon after. I spent the rest of my working life (before I got married) at the Co-op in Bury starting out at the corner of Garland Street and Looms Lane. I also worked at the first supermarket in the town, in Buttermarket, it was a Co-op self-serve and it had the Elite Café above; at times I was a relief in other Co-op stores in the town. I earned £3 10*s* a week and by the time I had given mum my keep I reckon I had just enough to buy a pair of stockings and a trip to the Odeon to see a film!

Sheila Collins née Walden (born 1937).

Earning Bread

I went to Culford School in September 1951. On leaving I worked for eighteen months at the Trustees Savings Bank in Hatter Street. After a short spell as a car salesman in Sudbury I came back to Bury to work as a trainee manager at Woolworths. One Saturday afternoon, the manager Mr Mandley called me into his office and said, 'I have a promotion for you; you start work in Biggleswade on Monday'. Well I went home and put my parts on telling mother and father I wasn't going; that finished my two-year career at 'Woolies'. However, that short-lived job stood me in good stead in my future line of business because a few months later I went to work at father's West End Bakery in Out Westgate, this was in 1963. I always liked meeting people and doing deliveries and bookwork though I can honestly say I was never a master baker like my father. We had seven vans on the road until 1974, when we finished deliveries so we could concentrate on the shop. That same year my previous work experience and contacts really came into play when the bakery landed a lucrative contract locally with Woolworths. I must say it was a pleasure doing business with them, no pressure or interference from head office and the manager was very fair. Once when a national bread strike took place, there was a severe shortage, we couldn't keep up with the supply and demand. The manager took our cottage loaves and split them in half; the bottom half sold as a large loaf the top as a small! When Woolworths stopped selling food in 1986 so did our agreement but we were still kept busy supplying other shops and hotels. Unfortunately due to pressure from the supermarkets, trade suffered as with all other businesses across the county. The West End Bakery closed in 2004. My love of cars, especially the Rolls Royce led me to acquire the number plate YLN 1, someone once said it stood for Young Looking Nigel, cheek!

Nigel Finch (born 1944).

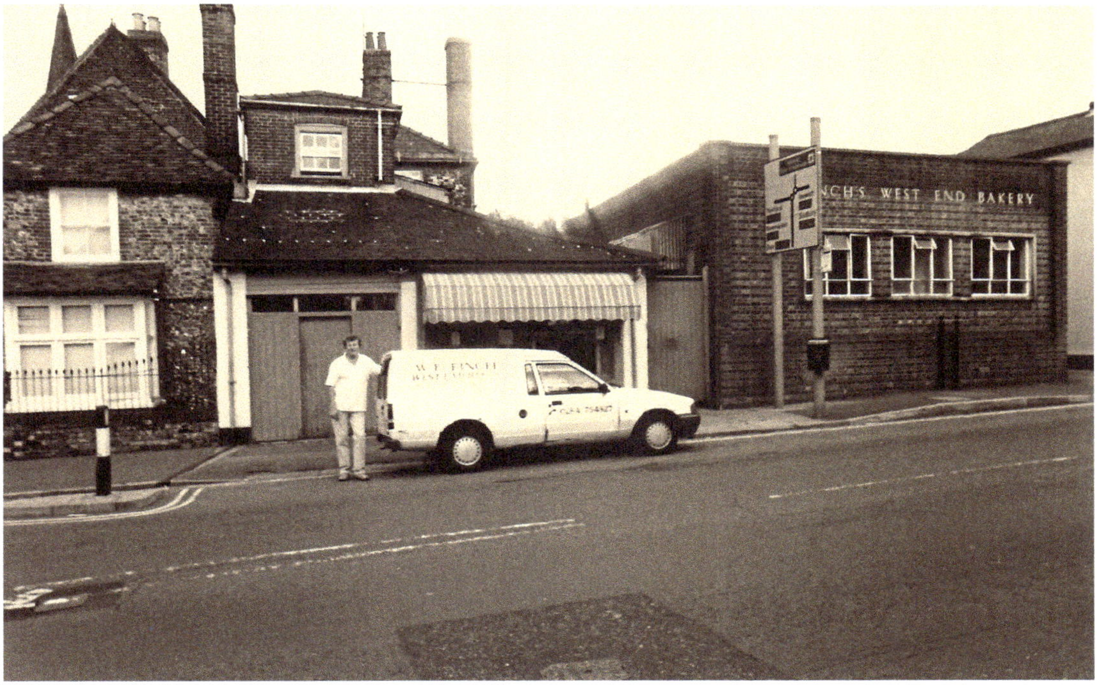

Nigel Finch with one of his delivery vans outside the West End Bakery.

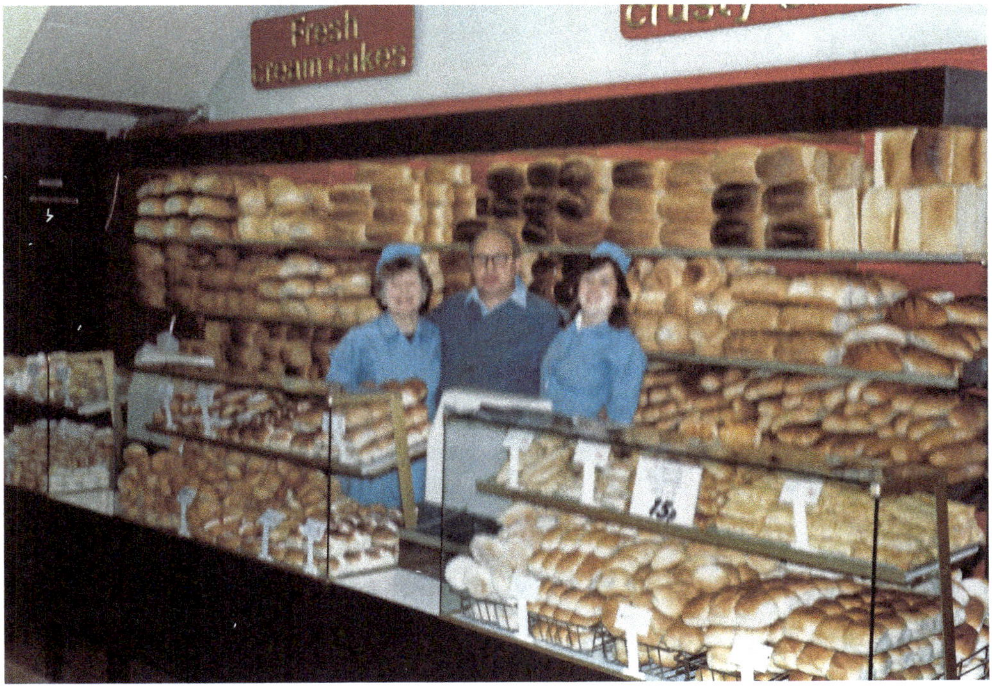

Woolworths bread counter.

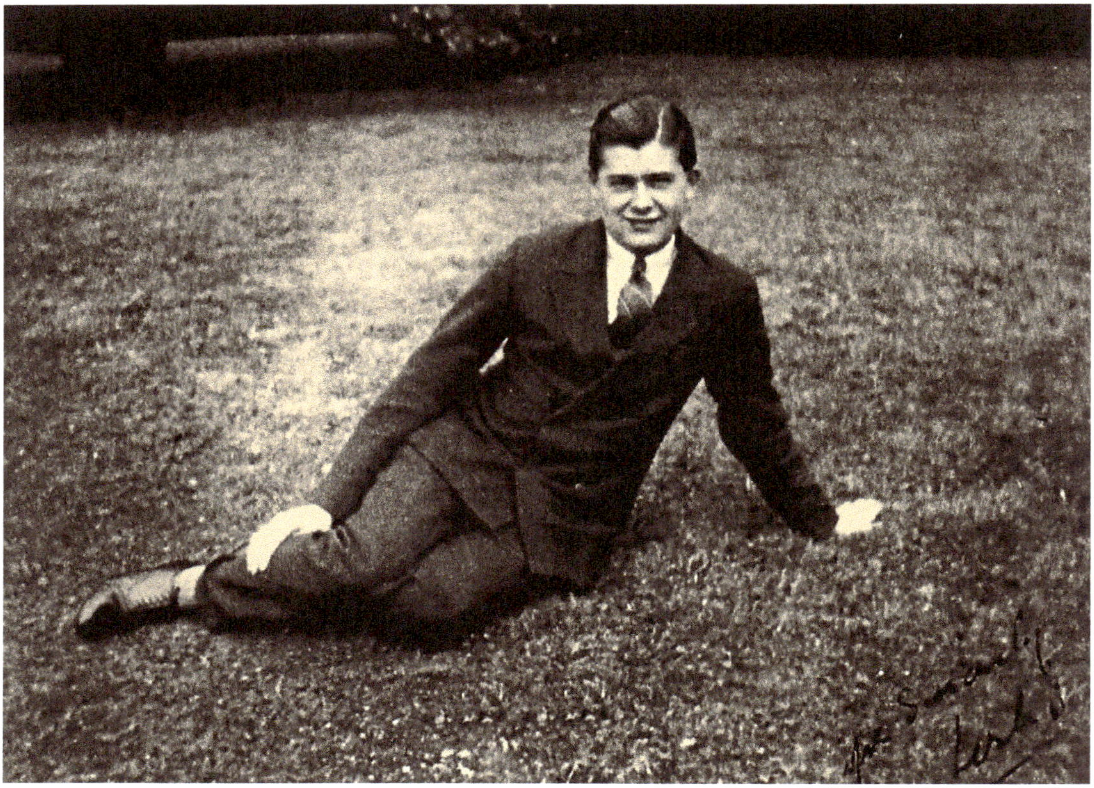

Leslie Jary in 1936.

The Reps

My father Leslie was butler to the 4th Marquess of Bristol, Frederick Hervey, for about fifteen years. However, when father returned after the war, life for domestic servants had changed forever. We had lived in Horringer but moved to Mitchell Avenue and dad became a telephonist, an amazing career move! He then bought Southgate Stores; I took to this life like a duck to water. I went to the Grammar School but I knew where my future lay and couldn't wait to get behind the counter. While at the Stores, Camay Soap was launched on commercial television with a big advertising campaign. Miss Camay, dressed in pink, visited the shop as my window display had won a competition! I saw the reps that came in, they all had big cars, the Kelloggs rep the biggest, the Brooke Bond tea man the smallest; he had a van like Postman Pats! Anyway I thought to myself I could do this repping, so for four years I worked for a couple of companies. I then opened a drug store on the Howard Estate in December 1967 and after ten successful years moved to the Nowton Estate, eventually ending up with my shop, Jaycraft, in Guildhall Street. This sold knitting yarn, etc. I relocated from there to St John's Street a few years later. I have always been involved in various local organisations as I believe what you receive in life so you should put something back.

Alan Jary (born 1944).

Calculations

After I got my qualifications, I joined the West Suffolk Council architects department that was on the top floor of Westgate House. I started as a copy typist progressing onto working on 'calculations' that were used in the bills of quantities that builders used to price-up tenders. There was a set of bells there that used to summon servants when it was a grand house. It later became Peatling & Cawdrons soon after the amalgamation of East and West Suffolk Councils in 1974. I had left before then going to Lewis & Marshall quantity surveyors in Northgate Street. I did everything about the office for three years before moving onto pastures new, The Martin Whitworth Partnership. As the architects for the St Edmundsbury and Ipswich Diocese, they were responsible for inspecting churches on a five-year cycle, I had to draw up the programme known as Quinquennial Reviews, I finished my working life there.

Beris Culyer née Walton (born 1944).

Compositing to Compost

I didn't like the Jubilee much, leaving there to start an apprenticeship as a compositer at the Bury Free Press. My dad was a bit disappointed as he had high hopes for me. In the terrible floods of 1968, I still lived at home in Horsecroft Road. I couldn't get to work through the flooding down by the Spread Eagle, but Len Hurrell, the composite room manager, sent the BFP delivery lorry to pick me up. When we got back to the BFP there was no power on so I had to turn around and wade back through all that water! After twenty years I was made redundant with the rest of the composite room staff. I had no other trade, so took up gardening for people, something I enjoyed and which kept me going till I retired.

Royston Crack (born 1946).

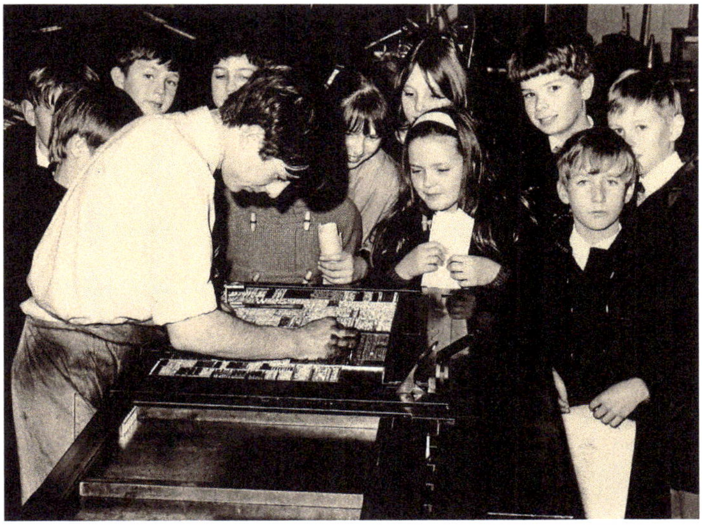

Royston Crack at the Bury Free Press showing children his skills.

Typing Skills

I was sworn in at Bury Magistrates' Court in 1958, becoming one of only two policewomen in the area. After two years' probation, my school typewriting skills came in very handy for typing up police reports; especially for three murder enquiries in the area when New Scotland Yard were involved. I had to pass a police driving test and point duty at the Butts Corner was a nightmare. I dealt mainly with women and children and road safety. On one occasion I went undercover at a bingo hall, wearing a wig to check if the gambling licence was being complied with. I won a Christmas pudding in their raffle but couldn't keep it. After eight years in Bury, I passed further exams and became a sergeant in Buckinghamshire and then an inspector in the Thames Valley police.

Olive Catton (born 1938).

Baker Man

My great-grandmother, Emma Childs had a café in Bell Arcade (Market Thoroughfare). My great-grandfather Daniel Childs had a bakery at 46, College Street, his son Oliver eventually moved it to 68, Guildhall Street during WW1; the bakery extended through to St Andrew's Street South. My father Claude Childs, Oliver's son had high hopes for me to join the family business and I was sent to Cambridge College and Technology as a bakery student in preparation for my future career although I wanted to be an engineer. After this, I did my National Service which consisted of spells at Padgate, Hednesford, and a fourteen week course at Henlow as an engine mechanic, I really enjoyed that time. I worked with my father for thirteen years and then on the sale of the bakery I got a job in the treasury department at Bury council as a rating officer, a post I held for thirty-one years and seventy-nine days, how about that for being precise!

Anthony Childs (born 1932).

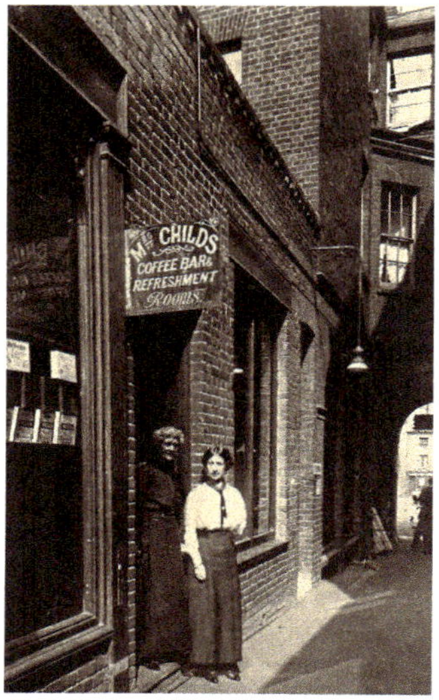

Anthony Childs's great-grandmother Emma on the left and his Great Aunt Lily outside their cafe in what is todays Market Thouroughfare.

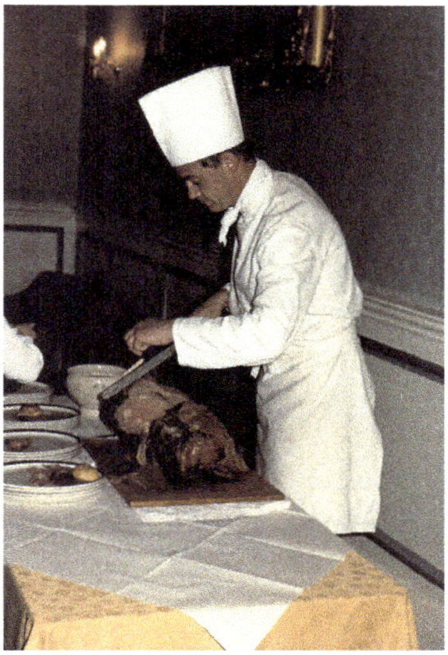

John Fulcher carving a joint of roast beef at The Angel Hotel.

Rôti de Bœuf

During the Second World War, my father won a Military Cross fighting in Northern Europe for which I am very proud. He was a butcher by trade; other uncles were involved locally in farming, funeral directors and a dairy. I went to Culford School and left to study catering at Cambridge Tech. After passing my exams, I worked in London as a trainee manager for Great Metropolitan Hotels, spending six months at Flemings Hotel in the West End. On occasions, I was in the kitchen and enjoyed the cooking side of it so much I decided that was the future for me. From there I went to Scotts Restaurant for three years, then the most famous lobster and oyster restaurant in the world. In 1973, my father sadly died and I came back to Bury and on the back of purely where I had worked in London got a job at The Angel Hotel. Within two months I was promoted as the Head Chef! Strange that, when you consider my forte was roast beef not seafood! I was there sixteen years before moving onto the Farmers Club retiring from the restaurant trade in 1991.

John Fulcher (born 1950).

A Heavy Fall

My first job was working for Harvey Frost builders as an apprentice carpenter. In 1949, there was a huge fire in one of the theatres at the old West Suffolk Hospital causing severe damage; afterwards Harvey got the job to do the rebuilding. I was working on the first floor one day when I must have tripped and fell against a fire escape door that opened. Unfortunately for me there was no staircase the other side and I fell to the ground below. I came to about a week later and was on crutches for a good length of time. I couldn't remember much about it all but one of the nurses thought I had come off my motor bike, which I strongly denied!

Brian Ransome (born 1934).

You Will Work There

At fourteen I saw a job advertised at Andrews & Plumptons, I went for it as I thought I'd be doing something in the workshop or similar. However, when I found out that the job was as an errand boy I told mum I wasn't going to take it. 'Yes you are' was the reply, and I did. I started on 10*s* a week but after eighteen months I finally got the job I wanted; in the workshop, but the pay was poor. I worked at Andrews & Plumptons till 1960; mind you I was better paid by then! I left and got a job with a subsidiary of The National Coal Board as a technical lecturer teaching domestic solid fuel heating. I got promoted to designing heating systems, troubleshooting, etc. The biggest problem I encountered was in 1985 when flue lining regulations came into force. Altogether I worked within the solid fuel industry (now British Coal) for thirty-four years.

Peter Dove (born 1927).

Fit for a Queen

I did several jobs before being called up including working at Suffolk Motors and Van Melles sweet factory. I did my basic training in Oswestry in Wales before going out to Germany in The Royal Artillery. Coming back to Bury I got a job on the water department at the council. When the Queen came to Bury in 1961, me and my mate, who was a plumber, helped put in a 'special rest room' in what was basically a tent near the Cloister Gardens. It had a carpet and washbasin and all that. Whether it was ever used who knows! Altogether I worked for the council for about thirteen years, even putting on the services for part of The Howard Estate where I now live. That council department became part of The West Suffolk Water Board, now Anglian Water.

Neville Waller (born 1939).

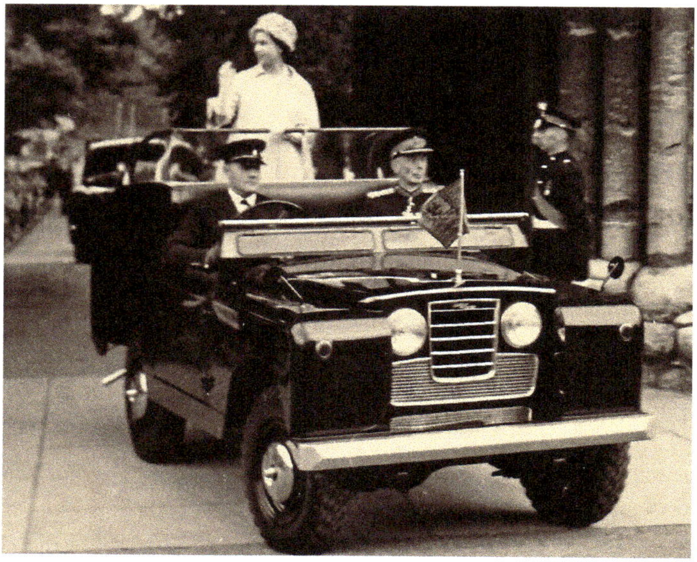

The Queen on her visit to the town in 1961.

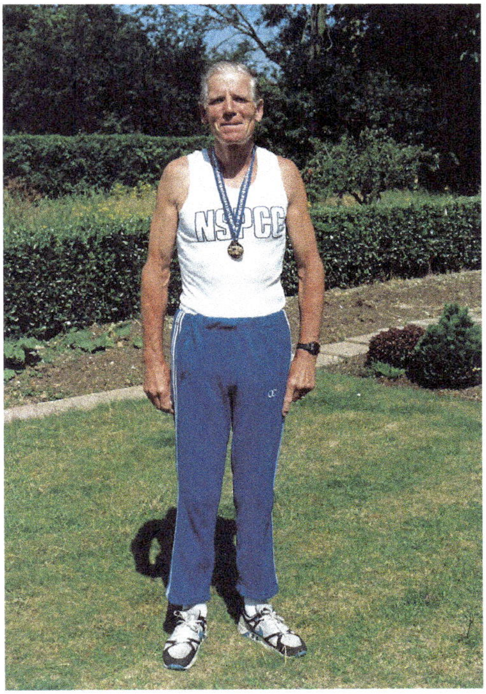

Michael Robertson Marathon Man.

Sleeping In

I was working at Bobys when it shut down for about a fortnight during the bad winter of 1947 because of power cuts. Anyway I turned up for work at 9 a.m. on Monday after the shutdown not realising that work had restarted at 8 a.m., the electric was back on, a fact advertised in the Bury Free Press. Unfortunately we never took it! My mother got 10*s* from my 17*s* 6*d* a week wages for my keep. My pay wasn't that clever, so I went to Watson's timber yard before becoming a van boy with Ridleys the grocers. I had been in Sea Cadets, so joined the Royal Navy, but only did nine months training at Shotley before being medically discharged. I returned to Bury and saw a film at the cinema called *How Green was my Valley* about coal mining. I thought that was the future for me and went up to Rotherham to do some training for the coal face before earning my first ever £5 note in my wages. However, something reoccurred that had followed me all my working life; I couldn't get up in the mornings! I came back to Bury and got a job for a short while for the gas board, my younger brother Dennis worked for them for years. After I got married, my dad said it would never last but it did for fifty-three years! I changed my errant ways working for Thomas Stewart civil engineers from 1964–69 in Western Way. One day a Polish bloke there asked me, 'Where do you come from as you don't sound English?' Can you imagine a foreigner asking me that! Strangely, the oddest thing for the last twenty-nine years of my working life I was a postman, which meant getting up early! When I was fifty-two I took up running, completing ten London marathons and raising money for charity.

Michael Robertson (born 1932).

Don't Knows

My mother Doris was a Stebbing, bakers of Northgate Street, the A14 access road is there now. I didn't like school and preferred working on the market stalls. I was put into 'The Don't Knows' at the Jubilee for those of us who hadn't a clue what we would do. I suppose I followed all the rest of 'The Don't Knows' into the building trade! I got an apprenticeship with builder Lennie Sewell. Most of my work then was building Rembrandt Way earning just £3 a week, rising to £7 after two years. I gave up my apprenticeship as my father Ernie suddenly died when I was seventeen years old. I became self-employed on the Friday and started back on Monday for Lennie, earning three times the money! I later went subcontracting on the Howard Estate for Hurstwood Construct. One of my passions then was motor bikes; I met with my mates either in Acacia Avenue, at The Butts or The Ipswich Arms trying to evade the police as they chased us around town. I went on to buy a plot of land out at Rede and built a house on it. With my girlfriend Anne, later to be my wife we lived on site in a caravan; I bought it for £25. I later sold it to a bloke from Chedburgh and he sold it to a hot dog vendor on Angel Hill. He cut off part of the side and I used to go by and say to myself 'I used to live in that!'

Roger Vickers (born 1948).

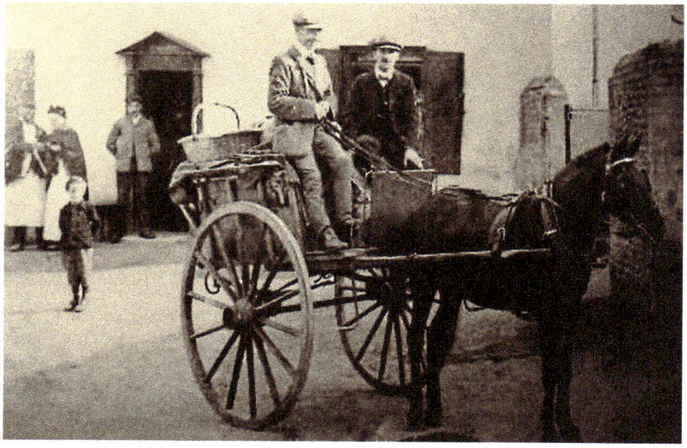

Edgar Stebbings in his pony and trap.

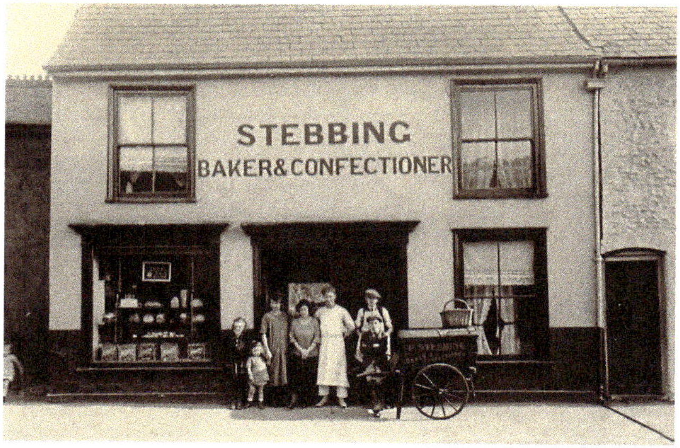

The Stebbings Bakery in Northgate Street.

Good Practice

I considered myself a better sportsman than an academic when I was younger, so when my uncle, Ernest Scott, who had an architect's practice in Bury, offered me the chance to be his pupil I said thank you very much! I never received any wages for over four years, relying on pocket money from my mother and a few shillings from my uncle to go to the cinema or whatever. As I took external RIBA exams to be an architect I was offered deferment from National Service. I toddled off to London in 1956 to work for Scheppes architects department returning in 1961, I was married by then. I was fortunate to be headhunted by The Mark Jennings Partnership of London, though they had an office in Bury. They wanted help on a brewery project in Wiltshire. I had lunch one day with their chief architect, agreeing a starting salary expecting it to be reduced, but two days later a confirmation letter arrived in the post with a higher figure. When I queried about it, I was told the sum offered was easier to divide by twelve, the number of months of the year! Sadly my uncle's partner became seriously ill and I was offered a position in the business even though I was still not fully qualified. Eventually I was made a partner, becoming a sole practitioner when my uncle retired.

John Abbott (born 1935).

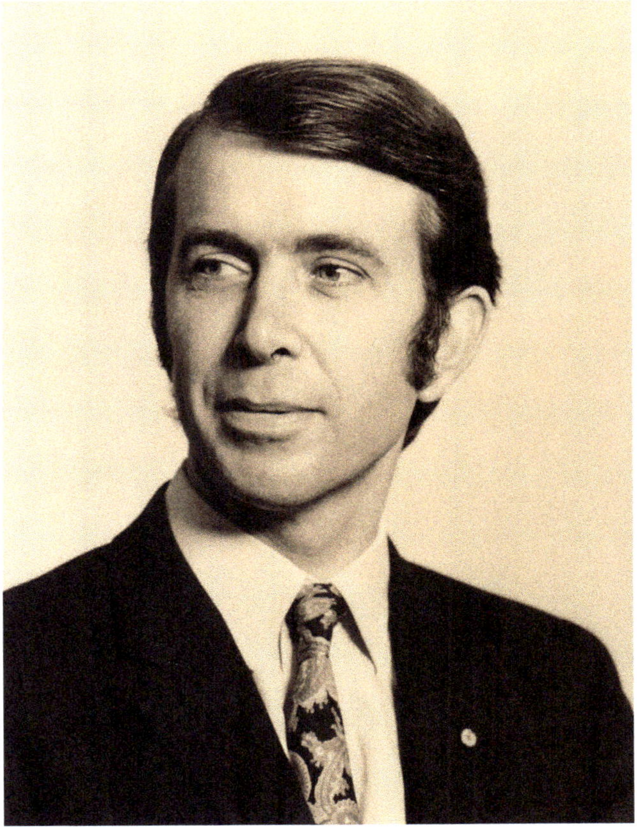

John Abbott architect.

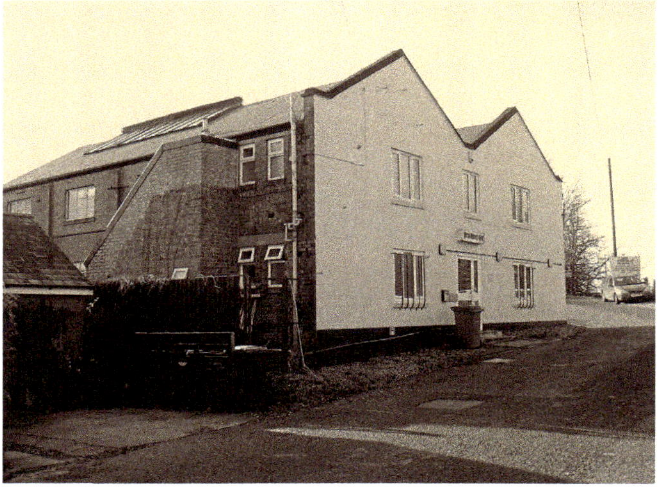

The former Douglas Warnes clothing factory on Thingoe Hill.

Impatient to Start Work

I wasn't quite fifteen when the Jubilee school term finished so I had to stay on longer before I could leave, though I did bunk off when I could in that 'extra' term. I started work at Douglas Warnes clothing factory at the top of today's Thingoe Hill as a machinist working mainly on sports shorts though other girls and women worked on outfits like Girl Guide and Brownie uniforms. I biked to work starting at 8 a.m. and finished at 6 p.m. with an hour for dinner and a tea break in the morning and afternoon. Sometimes during our break times we used to pop down to the little shop in Fornham Road to buy sweets and cigarettes. The youngest of us girls used to be given the job every Friday to go and collect fish and chips, the order having been phoned through in the morning though not everyone of the forty or so people who worked there had them. My wages then were £3 13*s* a week!

Christine Cook née Taylor (born 1944).

Early Brackland Years

My grandfather worked at Bobys on weaponry during the First World War but my father, Bob Burroughs, worked at the nearby Gasworks. The King 'Billy' pub (William IV) in Long Brackland could be seen from our house and soon as it opened dad was in there till closing time. I was one of three children and life for all the people around there was hard. After St John's Infants and St Edmundsbury, I went to the Silver Jubilee, leaving at fourteen. I got a job at Stetchworth Dairy in The Traverse waiting on tables in their café at the front. They had a dairy that backed onto Skinner Street. I then progressed onto the restaurant in the cellar where the better off in Bury used to pay five shillings for their meal! When the war ended a party with what we had was thrown in Long Brackland and we all danced in the street.

Phyllis Chapman née Burroughs (born 1930).

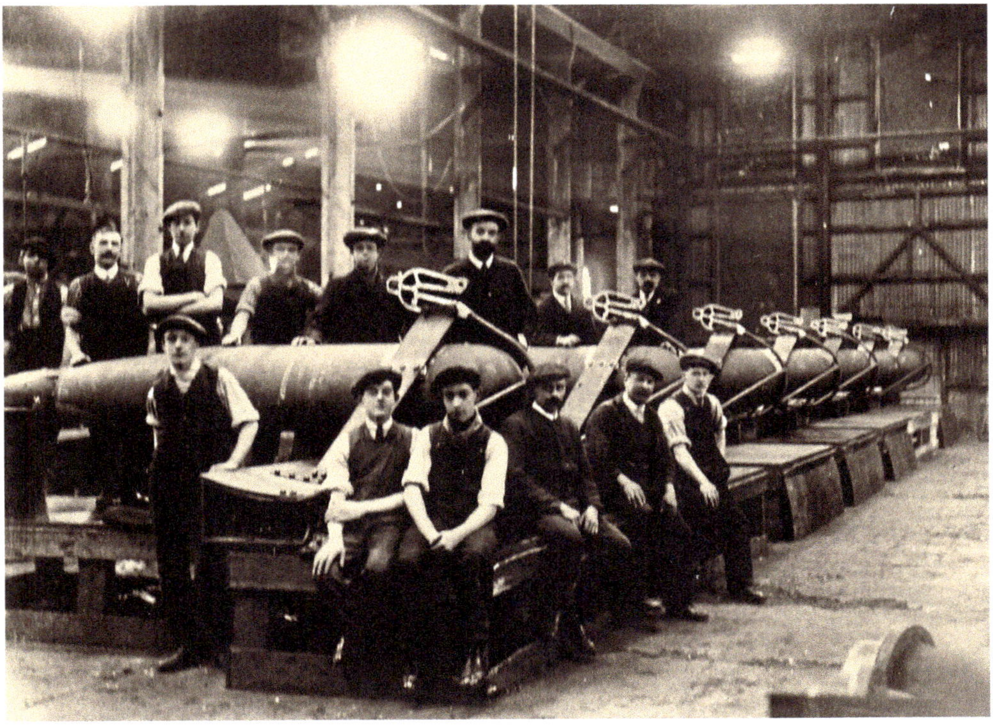

Bobys Factory in the First World War. Phyllis Chapman's grandfather is third from the right at the back among torpedoes.

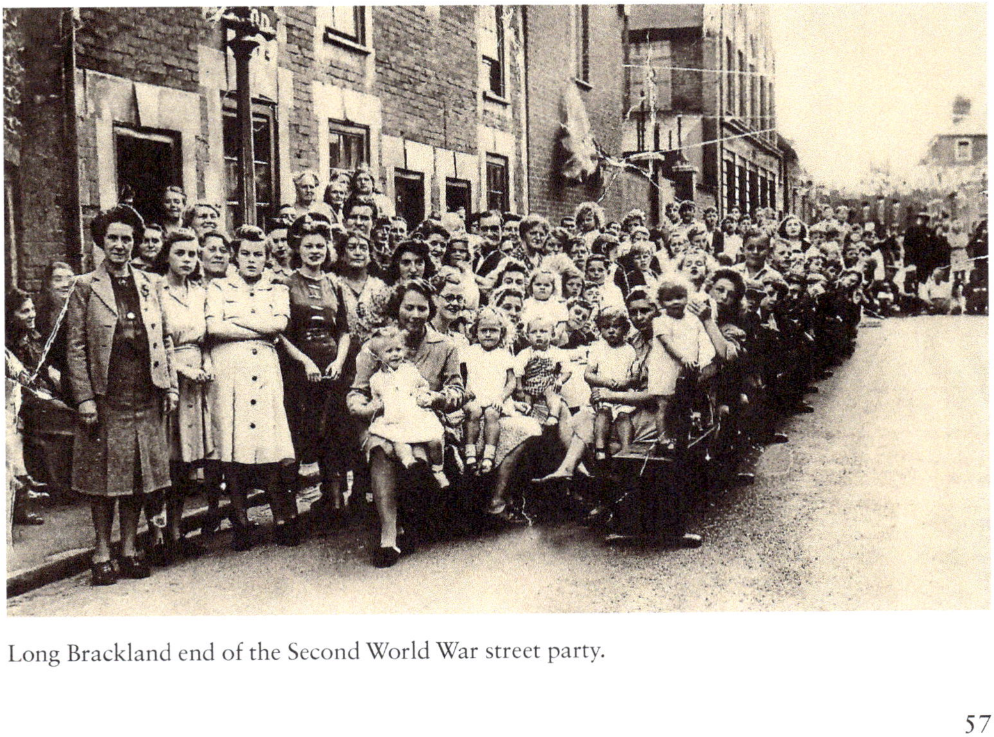

Long Brackland end of the Second World War street party.

A Builder's Life

My father Fred started his building business in 1928 after coming out of the army. A brave man, while in the Lincolnshire Regt, he won the Military Medal in the First World War for taking out a machine gun post. I was one of seven children and was born at fifty-one, Churchgate Street, where my father also had his yard. I helped my father in the holidays and at weekends. I left school at fifteen and went straight into the family firm. As a carpenter I worked alongside six tradesmen my father employed, many of whom had worked for F. H. Fenner for a number of years. I was called up and did my bit in the Pioneer Corps from 1955 to 1958, it was a cushy number. Coming out it was back to business as usual, going to work was a pleasure. We did lots of work for the Diocese, one job in particular on Little Saxham church required us to strip out the pews, lay a new floor and then put back the pews. All of us working there really enjoyed it. We left a block of wood there with our names on, hidden for future generations to find.

Bill Fenner (born 1936).

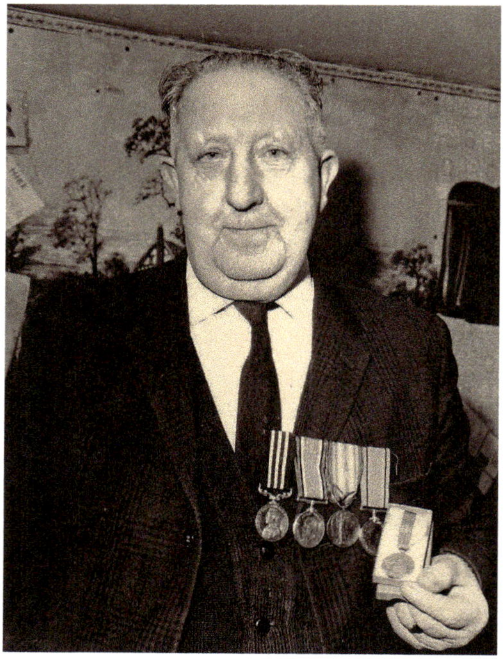

Fred Fenner proudly showing off his war medals.

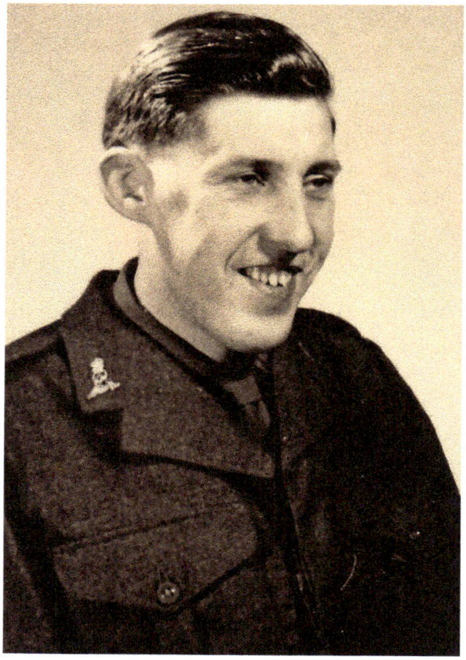

Bill Fenner during his National Service.

Pastimes

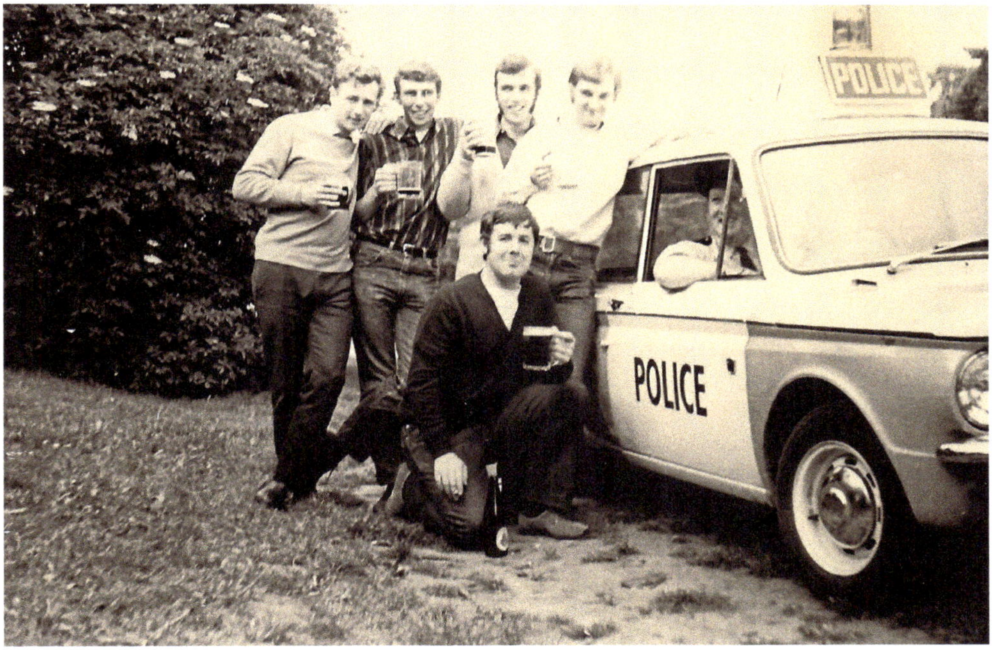

Best Mates: Colin Green on left, with Mick 'Bootsie' Segeant, Les Gibbon, Keith Baker and Peter Utting kneeling.

Fossil Hunting

When I was about seven, my father Neville Green won about £300 on the football pools, a lot of money then. Being brought up in a pub, he knew what he wanted to do with the money; he became landlord of the Blackbirds in Bridewell Lane in 1953 keeping it till it closed in 1973. The Blackbirds was very handy for me to go to the Feoffment School. Once we did an exchange visit with a school in Bury, Lancashire, comparing rural Bury St Edmunds with industrial Bury, we found them very different. I liked going field walking and on one day in a field, corner of Shakers Lane with Rougham Hill, I came across a beautifully worked crescent-shaped flint knife. This ended up in the British Museum, I got 10*s* from them for it! They thought it might have come from a royal burial mound; they even did an aerial survey of the site in 1958 but found nothing! I used the money to go and see the Bury pageant a year later. Around this time I also became interested in train spotting going down to Bury station. My mates and I used to get in the waiting room playing shove halfpenny on a long table there. The train interest came back later on in life.

Colin Green (born 1946).

Area Champion

I ended up at the County School leaving at sixteen, not because of ability but because my father paid the fees as he did for all my brothers and sisters. I had been in the Army cadets from the age of fourteen up at the Barracks. I was a drummer in the band there, even going on an army course at Colchester. At Blenheim Camp I liked training and boxing and went up to London to represent the cadets at The Royal Albert Hall as the Southern Area champion. Sadly I lost, but it was a great experience.

Ron Colson (born 1929).

The Box Game

I was brought up on the Priors Estate; everybody was in the same boat. The lads I used to hang around with made trolleys out of orange boxes and bits of prams, wheels were very collectable. Going down Cemetery Hill could be a bit hairy at times! We used to play a game in the street we called 'Box'. Basically a rectangle was drawn on the road using chalk, the kerb used to form one side of the box. A stick was laid from the top of the kerb onto the road. The object of the game was to stand outside the box, flick the stick up and thwack it up the road with a larger stick as far as you could. Whoever hit it the furthest was the winner!

Bill Pattle (born 1935).

Knocking About

I got called up signing on as a physical trainer and went into the Suffolk Regiment stationed at the barracks. One day my brother Sam was surprised to find me on our home doorstep wondering what was up. I told him I was expected to change in front of the other blokes something I had never done before, so I'd come home. Well, dad went potty and gave me a clout even though I was eighteen. Eventually I really liked the army; going out to Germany and Cyprus was exciting. After I came out around 1957, I went to work labouring up at the Sugar Beet factory, leaving there to go into the demolition game, knocking down places like Flittons fish and chip shop, The Odeon and The Kings Head. In the early 1960s, there were a lot of football teams playing friendlies on Sundays. I was involved in setting up the Bury Sunday League and ran Priors Utd, basically lads from the Priors Estate. We were one of the most entertaining and successful teams about. I also became interested in greyhound racing and was sad to see the Bury track close in 1996. Perhaps many people though can remember the Middleweight boxing match at the Athenaeum between me and George Bayliss. It was absolutely packed; George and I battled it out solidly for the three rounds, he getting the points decision. A long time ago now!

Joe Taylor (born 1936).

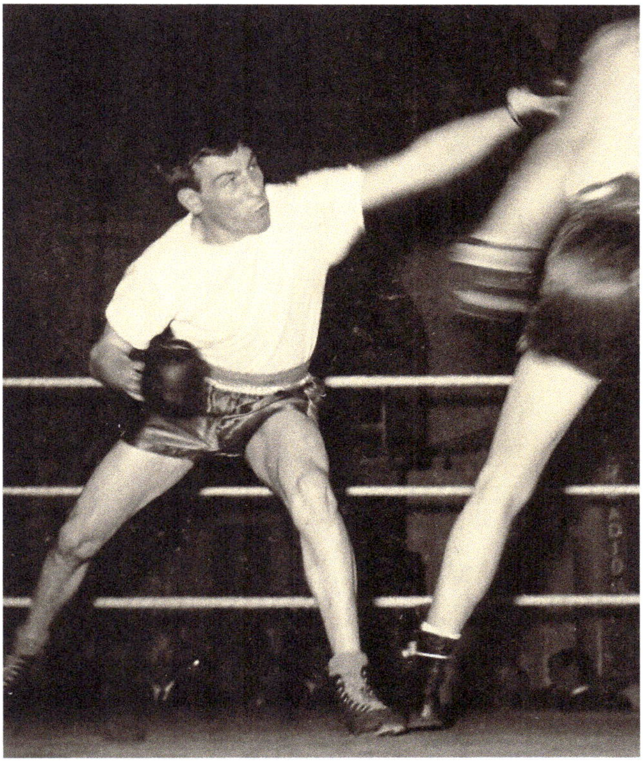

Right: Joe Taylor in his boxing days.

Below: Priors United Captain Joe Taylor receiving the Sunday League Division One KO Cup 1975–76 from Gordon Butcher.

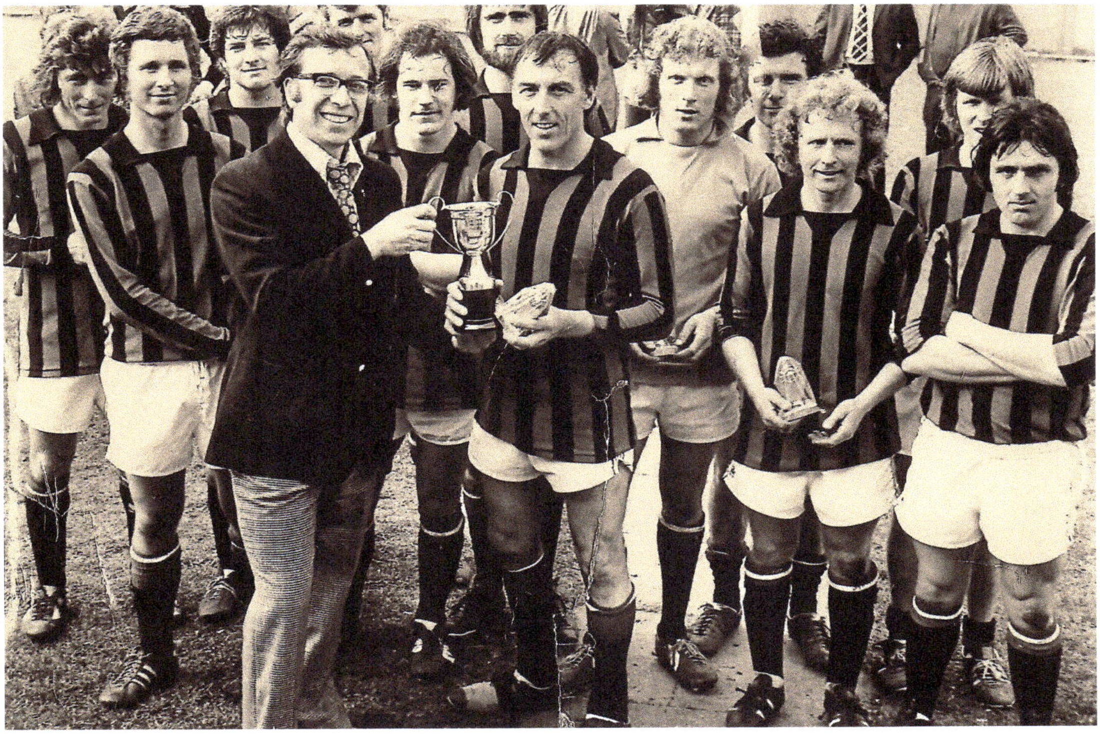

French Cricket

We were never bored as youngsters; there was so much to do. Tag was a great game running around the playground 'tagging' everyone till they were 'freed' by someone. Flicking cigarette or tea cards close to the wall was good fun. Winning increased one's own collection and the trading of 'swapsies'. Most of us kids played football no matter how bad a player you were; some even thought they were really good. Very competitive games were played down the Abbey Gardens or down the fields off Hospital Road often leading to mud-caked clothing for mums to wash. Summer was for cricket though I wasn't much good at it. We played 'French Cricket', where the batsman had to defend his or her legs from getting hit by a tennis ball thrown by an enthusiastic 'bowler'. In the winter slides were created on the ice-covered playgrounds each of us taking turns to see who got the furthest! Cuts and bruises didn't matter. One day I rode my bike recklessly through the flooded Butts wearing my Sunday best, the thrill of my feet level with the handlebars was shattered as I strayed into a dyke and was submerged. I am eternally grateful to my rescuer who definitely saved my life but the explanation to my parents did include a few white lies!

John Saunders (born 1948).

A Uniform Man

I enjoyed sports at school, athletics, cricket and football, later playing for Bury Town FC Minors and Reserves as a goalkeeper, Bob Kirk looked after us. One of my jobs was to clean the first team boots, drying, dubbing and checking their studs that were nailed on! I later became interested in refereeing, this was in around 1970. I passed the exam; Jack Lever who was a traffic warden in Bury was the training officer. I went on to become a Class One ref on the old Southern League, before retiring from active duty, becoming an assessor. These days I enjoy a good game of crib and participated in the Guards Association.

Bernard Taylor (born 1939).

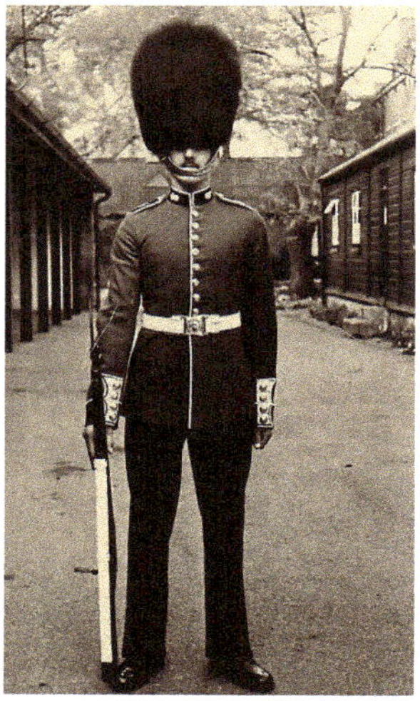

Grenadier Guardsman Bernard Taylor on duty.

Holding Court

There used to be a tennis tournament for juniors held every year at the Victory Ground, which was owned by Greene King. Mr Edward Lake, who was chairman of GK, had a sister called Miss Muriel Lake. She used to appoint the committee that ran it but she never really had anything to do with the actual work involved. However, on the days when play was on she would sit in a deck chair at the pavilion presiding over the event so when the players went in they paid their respects to her.

Jos Bird (born 1933).

Hot Stuff

After school, I used to go to Mr Baker, the blacksmith, who had a forge in St Andrew's St South around the corner from the Elephant and Castle. I used to like watching him and sometimes he would let me work on his small portable anvil he took with him while out shoeing horses. One day I was given a piece of red hot iron to knock into shape being told not to touch it as it was red hot. However, like a fool I picked it up when it had gone dark, boy did I burn my hand that taught me a lesson! Sometimes, I used to go up to the meadows near to where the old flax factory was and help father with his bees something I have liked doing all my life.

Roger Bruton (born 1944).

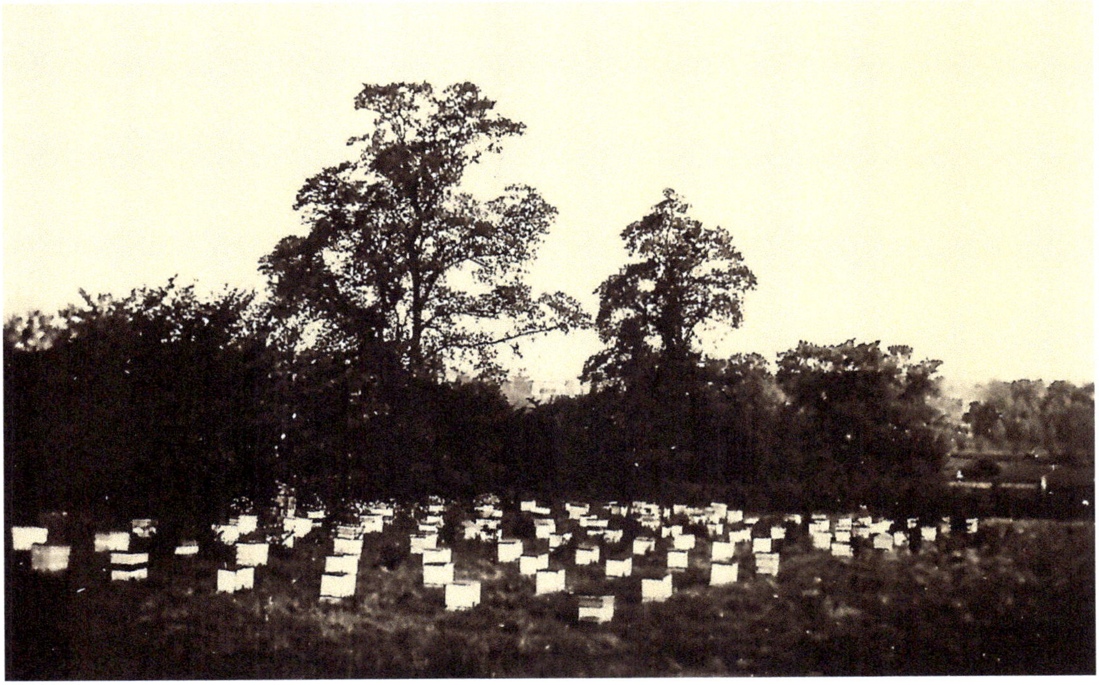

Beehives on the old Flax Factory meadows, now Cullum Road.

Early Morning Swimming Club

My father, Frank King, worked for the Corporation as a plumber during the winter months but during the summer months was preoccupied with his other job, swimming baths' superintendent on the playfields. He must have taught hundreds of children how to swim. There was a group of doctors who had their own season tickets; they used to go up to this open air swimming pool early in the morning to swim when nobody else was about. Some would arrive in their dressing gowns ready to go straight in!

Ann Pettit Née King (born 1954).

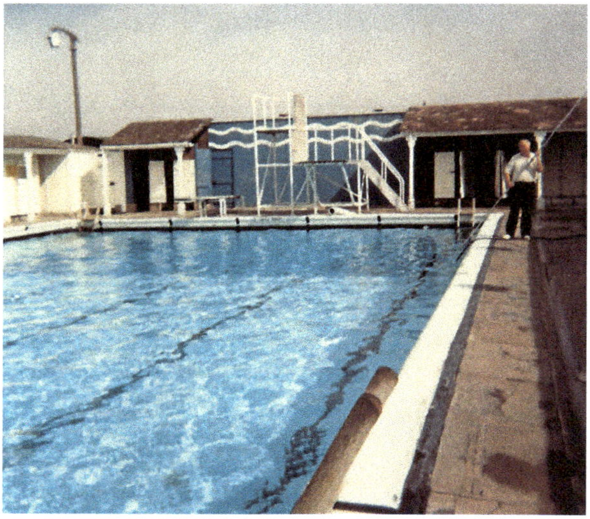

Left: Frank King on swimming pool duty at the playfields.

Below: Members of the Early Morning Swimming Club.

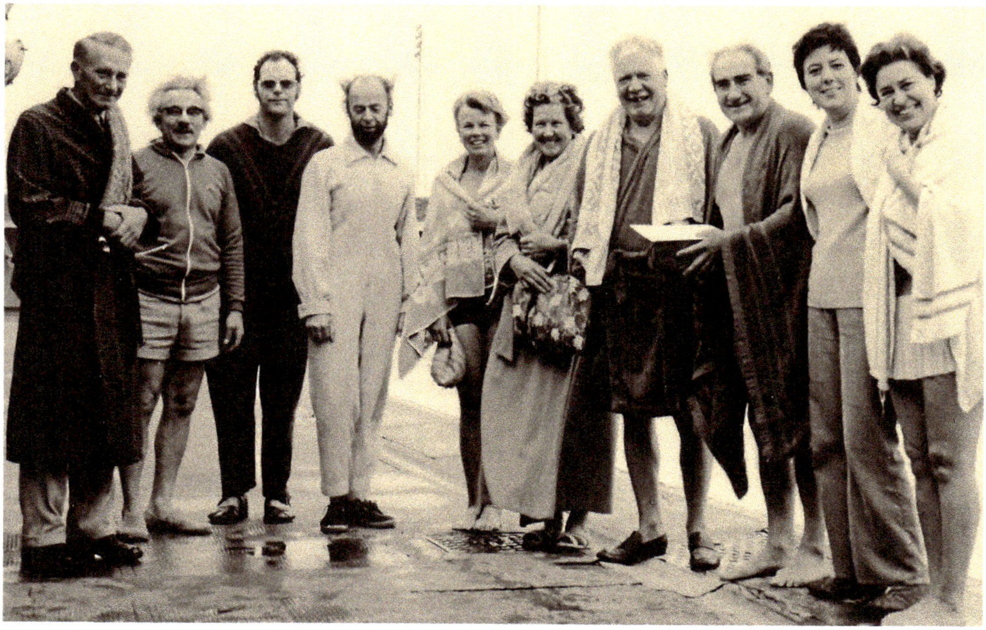

Nature Lover

Like all kids on the edge of the countryside (Mildenhall Estate) we played in the fields and down by the 'Coal River'. Opposite our home in Mitchell Avenue there were marshes and scrub land, this is all now covered with factory units; Haywards Pickles and a chicken factory were among the first to be built there, now long gone. We used to enjoy making camps, setting fires and bird nesting, everything we shouldn't have done. However this led me into a lifelong interest in natural history

David Addy (born 1948).

Make Hay while the Sun Shines

My friends and I loved going to pantomimes at the Playhouse and Saturday morning pictures at the Odeon. Sometimes I went up to Mount Farm and help with the haymaking there. My first job was at Finch's Bakery in Out Westgate though I also had a part-time job at Chinery's bookmaker corner of Churchgate Street and Guildhall Street. On the other corner was Mr Peachey's second hand shop; he had another further down the street next to the British Legion Club. I had been to dancing classes at Mrs Elliot's on Angel Hill opposite the cathedral so loved going to dances at the Athenaeum and the Co-op Hall in Risbygate Street, The Johnny Haines band played there. The bus station was in Brentgovel Street as was the White Lion; I had my wedding reception there. They and the Odeon are now gone. Also gone are The Maypole, Liptons and Woolworths, opposite 'Woolies' were three stands where the buses used to drop off and pick up for the three housing estates then in Bury. At Christmas when we were young the shops in Bury used to have competitions in the evenings and the town always felt so friendly, not like it is now with the ugly shopping centre and all the changes!

Margaret Beckwith née Johnson (born 1940).

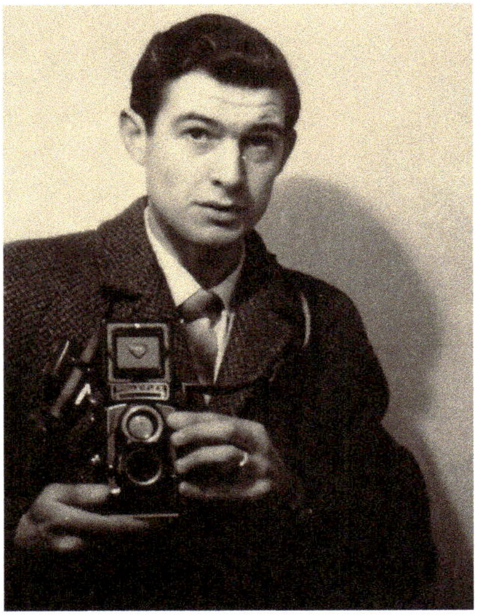

Richard Greene, keen photographer, aged twenty-two.

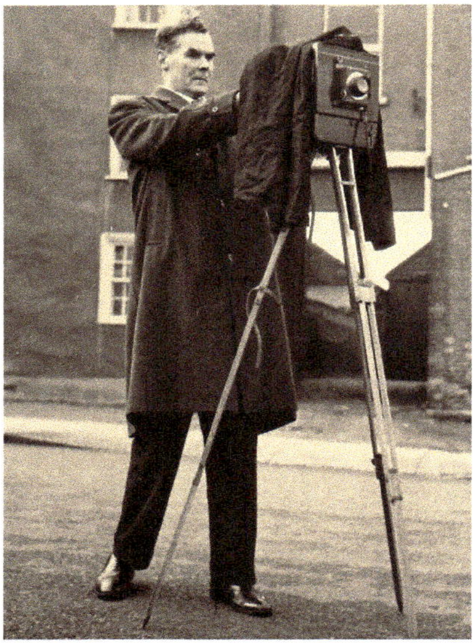

Oswald Jarman, photographer of Abbeygate Street.

Behind the Lens

I became interested in photography at an early age and when I was about fifteen I bought a camera made in Dresden called Kamera-Werk. It costed £16, purchased from Sneezums, which was a lot of money in those days. I photographed all sorts of scenes and people around Bury, one day even taking a picture of Oswald Jarman, the town's famous photographer. When the queen came to Bury in 1961, I snapped her and then the Duke of Edinburgh up at the Barracks. He was inspecting troops, and when the official photographers ran to get close-up shots, I ran with them! The camera I used most was again a German make, a Rolleiflex twin lens.

Richard Green (born 1939).

Jazz

My parents built a house on the Hand Laundry site and I lived there for about two years before going off to boarding school at Southwold. I eventually went to St Andrew's University, meeting Jim, my future husband there. We returned to Bury in 1961, the town had changed so much. Jim took over the running of the laundry, expanding it; however, in the evenings and weekends, he was involved with his great passion, Jazz. Friday night at The Sword in Hand in Southgate Street was always popular. My parents loved the Theatre Royal and were great friends of the Blackburnes of Nowton Court School who were great supporters too (my parents did the school laundry as well!). I, like my parents also have a great love of the theatre. I went back to science teaching part time when my children were older and have spent time working within the charity Relate.

Sheila Bayne née Forbes (born 1938).

Hula Hoops

I was twelve when I entered a hula hoop competition at the Playhouse. There were quite a lot of competitors, but being tall and thin I was quite good at it. I won, my prize was a box of chocolates. I was chuffed to bits! Four years later, I went on a coach trip to Yarmouth with a load of my friends and we ended up in the Garibaldi, then a very popular bar for music and dancing. There was a hula hoop competition on and my friends dared me to enter. I did, swinging two hoops on my hips, and won a bottle of champagne which we all enjoyed, there and then! As part of my working life I spent thirty happy years at the Bury Free Press as a photographic technician, initially in the dark room to working on computers. The BFP used to have a float in the annual carnival, in which many of us participated and had great fun.

Lorna Allen née Taylor (born 1946).

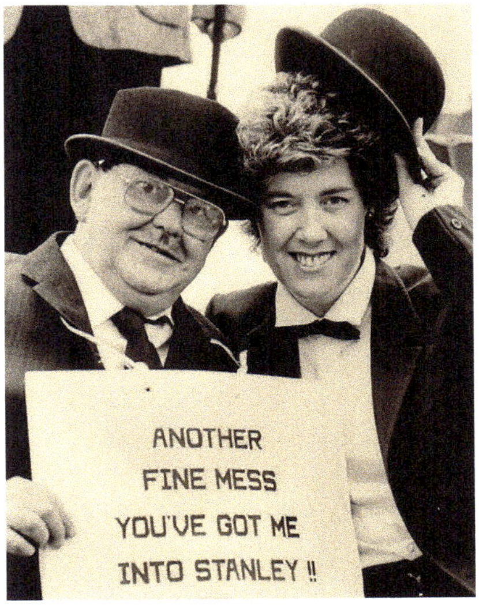

Lorna Allen in carnival mood as Stan Laurel with Oliver Hardy (not known).

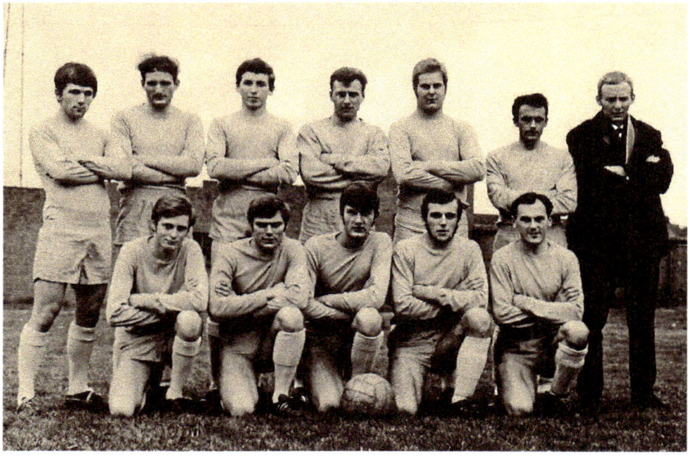

Bobys FC, 1967.

Football Passion

As a youngster, I was a keen sportsman playing cricket and football. When I was eleven, I realised that not many people wanted to play in goal so I became a goalkeeper. In my last day at the Silver Jubilee I played for the teachers against the boys! My working life started as an apprentice in 1961 for Bobys; a lot of people worked there. Some of my mates went to the St Edmunds Roman Catholic youth club so we helped clear out the crypt under the church. We formed a very successful football team celebrating fifty years in 2015. I married and went to South Africa in 1970, our proposed two-year stay ended up as over five! Unfortunately things didn't work out for us and we returned in 1976. As Bobys had finished, I went to work at Barber Greene until it closed in 1988. My most memorable moment in football was in 1972 playing in the Johannesburg football stadium for Wanderers FC winning the Transvaal Cup, equivalent to the English Amateur Cup something you would never have dreamt of doing.

Colin Green (born 1946).

Football Mad

My first real competitive game was aged fourteen for Bury Town 'A' in the Bury & District League. From there I played for Bury Reserves at their Kings Road ground. Off and on I played for Bury for the next twenty years with spells at Haverhill, Soham, Stowmarket and Thetford, whom I managed at one time in 1981. One of my career highlights was playing at Portman Road, Ipswich in the Suffolk Premier Cup final against Ipswich Reserves although losing. I enjoyed playing for local teams like Gazeley and Priors United with huge crowds watching local cup finals. Injuries were treated very differently then, if you hurt your ankle you put it alternatively in buckets of cold and hot water then rubbed some 'horse cream' into it and hoped that sorted it out!

David Hoggett (born 1947).

Coaching

My father on retiring from Bury Town FC took on The Butcher's Arms in King's Road, which enabled me to play for Westgate Brewery FC and their cricket team. Herbert Hargreaves, a former Yorkshire cricketer, was the groundsman at the brewery owned Victory Ground and he took me under his wing when I was about thirteen, he was a lovely man. I progressed further and was chosen to play for Suffolk in the Gillette Cup against Kent one of the top County sides then. At one time we had them at 40 for 3 but then Colin Cowdrey came in and knocked up over a ton that was my first experience of first class cricket! As time went by Greene King sold the Victory Ground to St Edmundsbury Council and it was left to several dedicated people including myself to set about ensuring its future. Victory Sports Ground Ltd was formed in 2000 and a thirty year lease obtained. When I retired from active cricket I became a fully qualified coach eventually mentoring other coaches some who are at first class cricket clubs.

Bobby Flack (born1943).

Playing for a Good Cause

All through my life I have enjoyed sport, especially football, from my first game for Sicklesmere FC aged fourteen. I took over running it in 1972; they were in division four of the Bury & District league then. I ran them for seventeen years till they finished in 1990 due to a lack of players and enthusiasm. Perhaps the game that stands out for me the most is a charity game in 1985 that I help organise between Sicklesmere and some of the cast from the BBC soap, Eastenders including Nick Berry. It was a fund raiser for the family of Garry Buckle, one of our players who sadly died of cancer at the age of twenty-seven. Played at Ram Meadow, home of Bury Town a lot of money was raised including some for Cancer Research.

Richard Mortlock (born 1946).

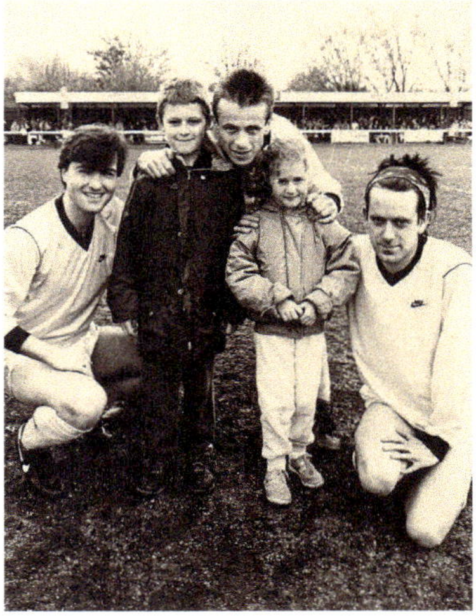

Eastenders stars from 1988. From the left, Nick Berry (Wicksy), Tom Watt (Lofty) and Chris MacHallem (Rod) with Keith and Alison Buckle.

Bells and Bowls

I learnt how to ring church bells while living in Coventry and have rung regularly at St Mary's church, Rougham. Currently I am the Vice Chairman of the Parochial Church Council and over the years have organised grants for essential repairs to the church. My wife Elisabeth and I joined the St Edmundsbury Bowls Club in 1975 and I still play there. Later I joined the Risbygate Bowls Club bowling during the winter. Retiring from work in 1995, I made enquiries about becoming a Blue Badge Guide in the town having always been interested in history and meeting people. I qualified as a guide in 1997 and am still guiding today.

Brian Coley (born 1939).

Aching Feet

Our home was No. 7, Horringer Road, which was always getting flooded, we eventually moved to Out Westgate. I had a wonderful childhood and often would walk with my parents to the Six Bells in Horringer on a Sunday evening. My first school was St Mary's Infants, opposite the Dog & Partridge, in Crown Street. I left school at fourteen wanting to work with children so I went as a nursemaid for two little boys in Northgate Avenue, it lasted a year. My next job was as a shop assistant at Dunns Restaurant in Abbeygate Street, which I had until war broke out. I went to all the local dances, which I thoroughly enjoyed, so much so that I would go home late at night with my high heels tucked under my arms as my feet ached so much. My father would stand at the top of the stairs and say 'where the hell have you been at this hour of night!'

Eileen Fuller (formerly Jennings) née Tooke (born 1920).

Almost a Local

Holy Ground

Dad was a fireman in Islington, London, for over twenty years. We all moved here as his experience was much needed in Bury. I was seventeen years old, a terrible age to loose contact with all your mates. I did several jobs including working as a labourer on the building of The Vinefields. I couldn't settle down and went back to London following in dad's footsteps by joining the fire service but it wasn't for me and I left a year after doing my training. I returned to Bury in about 1965 and met new friends. In those days there was a lot going on in Bury, dances at the Athenaeum and Co-op Hall in Risbygate Street also skating and wrestling at the Corn Exchange. I liked to go to the gym at Blenheim Camp doing weight lifting and boxing. One day with friends Terry Lilley and Roy Todd we were cutting across the Barracks parade ground on our way through from Beetons Footpath. A booming voice shouted, 'What the hell are you doing', it was an army sergeant. We ignored him as we said to ourselves we aint in the army. Then as if a voice came out of the clouds he bawled out, 'What do you think you are doing walking on God's holy ground'. We froze on the spot and he then told us more politely you didn't walk across the parade ground. In future we always walked around it!

Keith Hatton (born 1945).

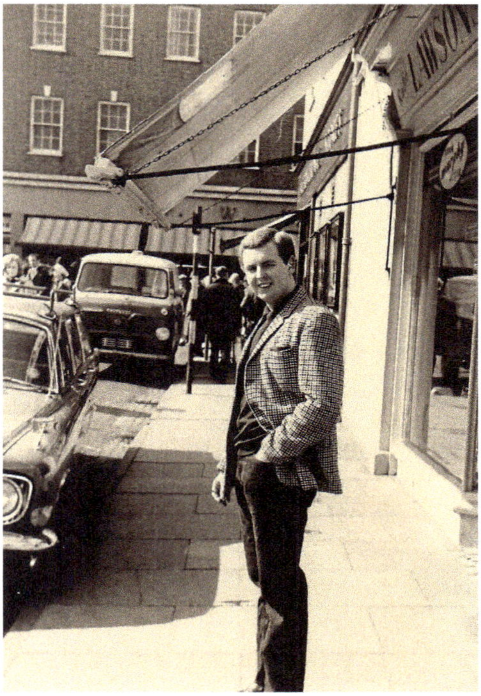

Keith Hatton, man about town.

Environmentally Friendly

Though born in Wrexham, I grew up in Kettering, leaving school and joining the Public Health Department of the local council as a junior clerk. During my National Service with the RAMC, I trained as a hygiene assistant based in Kent inspecting barracks in the area. Having studied at Canterbury Technical College and completed the first two years of an Ordinary National Certificate in building construction. After leaving the army I returned to Kettering and trained as a Public Health Inspector, qualifying in 1961. Then worked in Nottingham and in Coventry before moving to Bury St Edmunds in 1966 where I got a job on the Borough Council. Now married to Elizabeth, life in Bury was more sedate and house prices surprisingly comparable to Coventry. The year 1974 saw the formation of St Edmundbury Borough Council, my professional name being altered to Environmental Health Officer. My responsibilities included the inspection of meat, poultry and food preparation premises and abbatoirs. Being involved with 'slum clearance' and improving properties I found my ONC was very handy for this! Places I remember coming down were St Edmunds Place and Priory Cottages near the Tollgate. The emphasis on improving properties meant I was also involved with grant applications. Later I was responsible for various types of pollution control. I was promoted to Chief Environmental Officer retiring in 1995.

Brian Coley (born 1939).

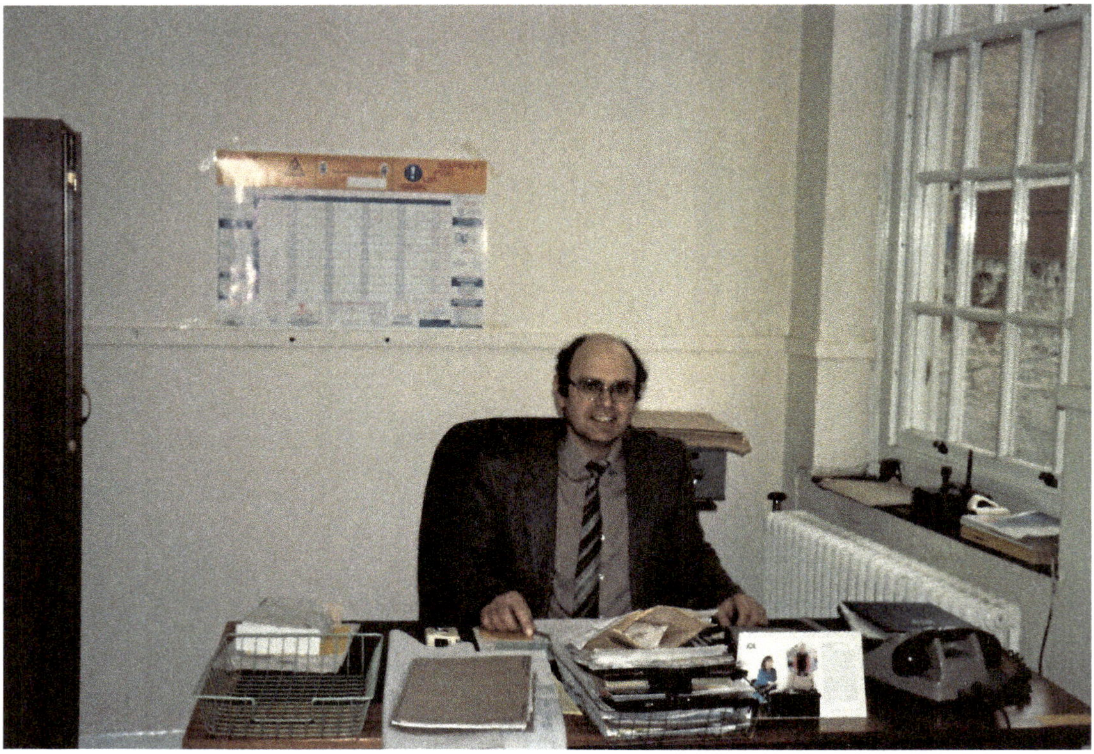

Brian Coley at work.

A Real Buzz

Born in Flempton, I attended its school till I was eleven. Mother was a Geordie who met my father when down here in the land army. Dad worked as a carpenter for Greene King. After the Jubilee I was an apprentice upholster at Copelands, leaving at twenty-one. The next two years I worked for Goffs Gallery in Whiting Street mainly on restoration. It was a super job but as I was looking to get married, I left to go to GK and more money. I became the Third Man in the Brewhouse, milling, mashing, hops weighing, etc., everything that made it tick. I volunteered to join the brewery fire brigade, which was affiliated to the Suffolk & Ipswich Fire Service. After going on some training courses I was as they say 'fit for duty'. Although I wasn't a retained fireman I still got paid the same on a call out. As a backup service to the 'big boys' we were nevertheless still very professional and attended some really big fires in the area. I attended the disastrous Bury Sports Centre fire in 1980, which was gutted, one of several arson attacks in the area that curiously always seemed to happen on a Thursday evening. Perhaps the biggest fire on Greene King's own doorstep was in the electrician's shop that had just had a new roof put on. I was working on a shift then and although I connected a hose to a hydrant, I didn't help in the fire-fighting as officially I wasn't on duty. I ended up as a leading fireman. When the GK fire service finished on 31 December 1997 I had been involved with it for twenty years; I got a real buzz from it.

Peter Baldwin (born 1950).

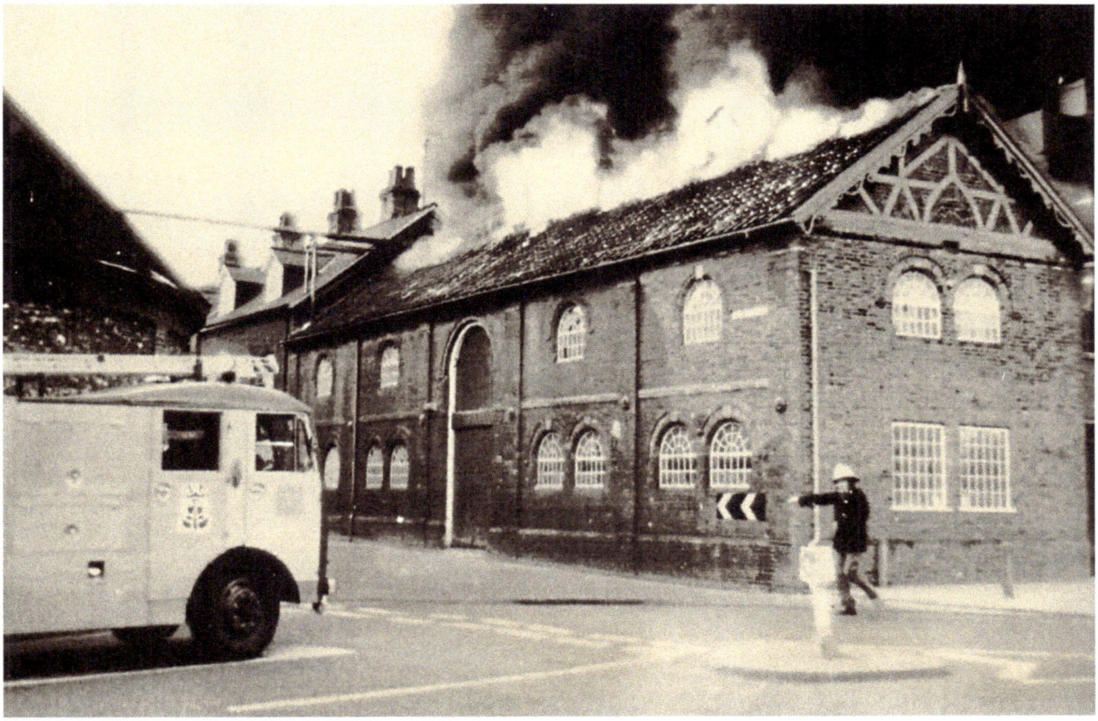

Fire at Greene King's electrician's shop, 1979.

Fancy Dress

My first home was in Pakenham. My father James 'Jubilee' Bluett was a dealer but also did fruit and veg; he was a cripple and once was caught driving a car on a learners licence out at Tostock. When taken to court he was fined £1, however, the police and magistrate were sorry for him. The *News of the World* paper wanted to print it but dad said no; he could have made a lot of money from it. My mother Mary was the daughter of the road sweeper in Pakenham whose surname was Sexton, I can't remember his first name but he always wore a collar and tie and bowler hat! They lived up by the Pakenham windmill. Mother never forgot my birthday as she always knitted me socks for it plus the day I was born she had been into Bury to get some new false teeth! We moved into Bury to live on Hill 60 (Priors Estate). Here, aged ten, I won a fancy dress competition that was held to celebrate the Silver Jubilee of George V.

Spencer Derek Bluett (born 1925).

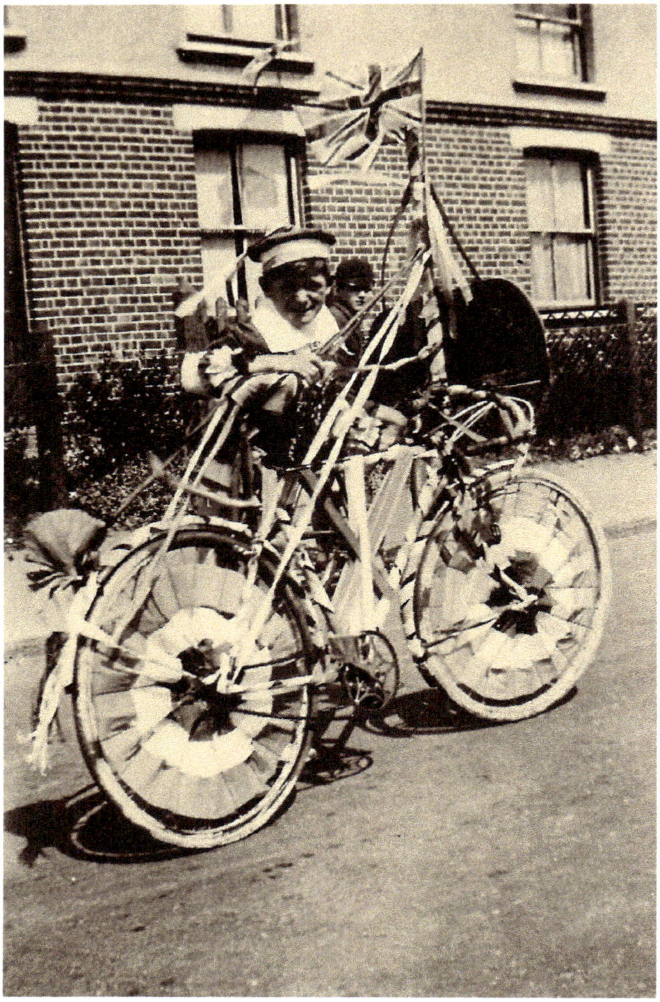

Derek Bluett aged ten with his decorated cycle.

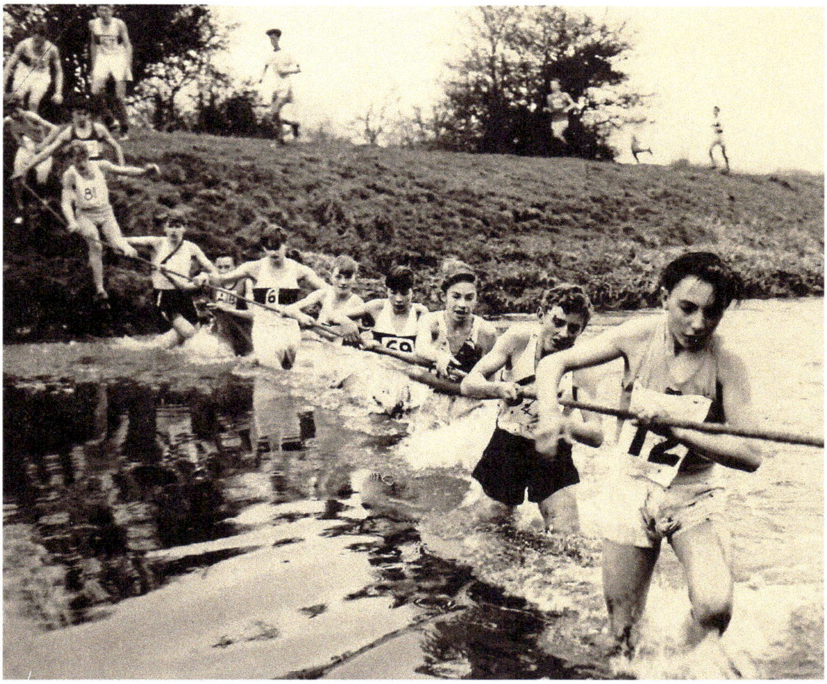

Richard Mortlock, third from right, on his way to crossing the River Lark.

Across Country

The early part of my life was spent in Little Welnetham. During the war my father had been in the home guard in Bury something of which I am very proud. I attended Great Welnetham School and at the age of eleven we moved just down the road to Sicklesmere. After passing the Eleven Plus Exam I went to the Grammar School in Bury. These were the days of 'winkle picker' shoes but we weren't allowed to wear them; toe-capped shoes were the order of the day. However, as soon as the opportunity arose, it was the 'winkles' on, fag lit and up to Purdys! I used to love cross country running, I considered myself quite good at it. At school the subjects you took were to some extent decided by the quality of the master taking them. I never attended the nasty teacher's lessons; you were more likely to get on with someone who made it interesting. Coming up to leaving school I had no idea what I wanted to do finally joining West Suffolk County Council after getting the necessary qualifications as a trainee civil engineer. Training for this post meant going up to Nottingham Polytechnic on a four-year course. I didn't participate in a lot of sport then but did do a lot of drinking as most students did! I passed my exams and became a fully qualified civil engineer working on mainly roads and bridges until West Suffolk CC merged with East Suffolk CC in 1974. I was rankled by the fact that the East Suffolk lot then got paid the same level as us but we had to pay for our travel back and forth to Ipswich! I left Suffolk CC in 1984 and then worked for several different civil engineering companies.

Richard Mortlock (born 1946).

A Fair Cop

By the age of four I had experienced life at Boxford and Long Melford where I was born. My father was a police inspector and in 1952 we moved into one of the police houses in Hospital Road. After St Peter's Infants, The Guildhall Feoffment and then St Edmunds Catholic School I transferred to the Silver Jubilee because of overcrowding in the senior class in 1963. By then our family lived in Queens Road. My upbringing was influenced by my mother's strong religious beliefs and I spent a lot of time at St Edmunds church, an institution steeped in history and interesting characters and something I am still heavily involved with. This ethos served me well as I progressed through life and in my subsequent career as a police officer. Although I worked away from Bury from 1965 till 1980 I enjoyed regular contact with family and friends when I came 'home'. When the time came to finally settle down in 1980 I had no desire to live elsewhere than Bury St Edmunds.

John Saunders (born 1948).

Well, Well

I came to Bury when I was twelve in 1940 from Sheffield. My father Norman Garside Chapman was a National Service Officer for the Ministry of Labour in control of labourers, mainly Irish. They worked on Airfields, something I also did for the first eighteen months of my working life. From there I went to Fulchers Dairy in Whiting Street, eventually meeting and marrying Phyllis in 1950. I did a plumbing apprenticeship for local builder Lennie Sewell, becoming self-employed in 1954/55. While apprenticed I worked at Lennie's house, Hardwick Manor. One day a submersible pump in the 116-foot deep well, which then supplied the water to the house, was playing up. One of the chaps Lennie employed cut the cable to it. When the electric company came to sort out what the problem was, they went ballistic as a new cable had to be put in!

Ted Chapman (born 1928).

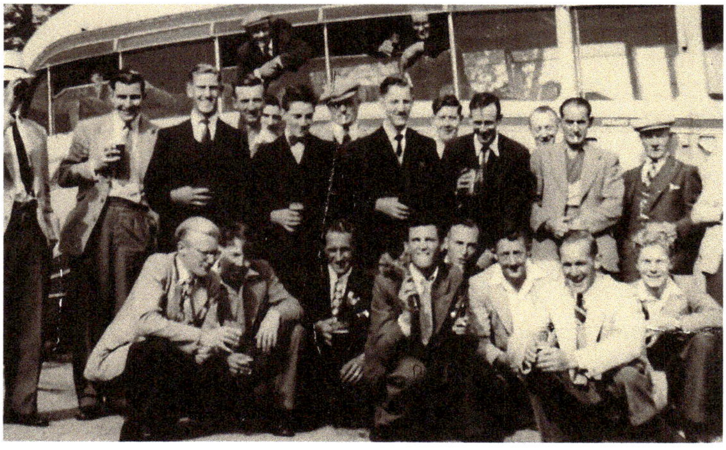

Ted Chapman, second on left kneeling, at Lennie Sewells firm's outing 1947.

The Deep End

I was born in North London; father was a salesman for an engineering company. I was sent to Culford School at the age of eight on the recommendation of a family friend. At Culford I travelled via steam train to Liverpool Street and vice versa. On approaching the now-closed Higham station between Newmarket and Bury us lads would lean out of the window and shout 'who's a fool?' just before the stationmaster shouted 'Higham!' We did everything boys did then, ice skating on Culford Lake and letting off flashbangs on bonfire night, occasionally getting the cane as warranted! The Culford Upper Fifth Removed of 1954 still holds reunions, the 60th in 2014. On leaving school, I did a three-year apprenticeship with an engineering company in Chelmsford, before joining the family business in 1959. HRP was started by my father in 1945 (seventy years in 2015) in Mitcham, Surrey. Because of the Culford connection father looked in Bury for new premises as the Mitcham site was being redeveloped. Firstly renting at the old Flax Factory and then moving to the old bottling plant of Hunters & Olivers in St Andrew's Street South. Sadly my father died in 1963 and I was thrown in at the deep and ended up running a wholesale commercial refridgeration and air conditioning company. I realised the company could grow and in the subsequent years after my father's death expanded the company developing a network of sales and distribution with its headquarters now at Rougham.

Kingsley Curtis (born 1937).

Serendipity

I was a pupil brewer for two years at Morrells Brewery in Oxford. In 1952, I applied for two jobs; the second at Greene King was successful, I had never heard of Bury St Edmunds. I got some wonderful digs on Angel Hill with Mrs Hodges, widow of Canon Hodges. I was left with about seventeen shillings a week from my salary by the time I had paid her £4. It was a good job my father subbed me an extra pound a week. Mind you they were worth it, breakfast, lunch and supper provided and during the summer on Saturday and Sunday, afternoon tea; beef dripping on toast in the winter! I was in Bury for about four years before emigrating to Canada but returned after three. I called in at Greene King's offices on a Saturday morning; they used to be open then, and I was interviewed and I had a job providing head brewer Bernard Tickner would work with me, he did! I had always been interested in amateur dramatics and played Charley in a production of Charleys Aunt at The Playhouse in 1955, it had been premiered in Bury in 1892. In 1970, I became Director of The Theatre Royal for twenty-five years. I had a career move, now married, my wife and I had this revolutionary idea of opening a shop that sold canework, glass, fabrics, etc., a complete departure from the norm in Bury. We called it Serendipity a name meaning finding nice things in unusual places. We had the shop twenty-seven years encountering lovely people and enjoying every minute of it. I think Bury St Edmunds has always been a wonderful place and is a happier place to live in now.

Paul Lainchbury (born 1933).

A Wonderful Place

A Plymouth girl, I started working life as a scientific assistant at the Atomic Energy Authority in Amersham. I met my husband Andrew who was on a six-year veterinarian course at Cambridge University. We got married with two years of his course to complete, living in Grantchester. He qualified and we came to Bury St Edmunds in 1967; he joined a practice in Cotton Lane, with the planned intention of staying two years. However unplanned children quickly followed and we decided to stay. The practice blossomed and my husband became a partner until his early death, in 1978, aged thirty-five. I moved from our home at West Stow Hall and have lived in town more or less since then. One of my most enjoyable times was running a successful B&B in Bury and I have found the town the most wonderful place to bring up children as a single mother!

Elizabeth Barber Lomax (born 1943).

Fornham Fun

My parents lived in Old Hall Lane, Fornham St Martin, dad worked on Colonel Long's farm all his working life. My brother Conrad and I used to love the freedom to be able to do just about anything you wanted to do then; blackberrying and rabbitting at harvest time were our favourites. I can just about remember some of the soldiers who were stationed at Fornham Hall. They were from the Highland regiments and a couple of their wives were billeted with us. When I attended the Jubilee I had to bike there, often encountering flocks of sheep being driven to Bury market. I left school to work in the fabric department at Prettys in Buttermarket though funnily I attended evening classes at the Jubilee doing dressmaking! Mr Hook, Prettys' manager always called me 'Sputnik' as I was always dashing about!

Pearl Burroughs née Wisbey (born 1940).

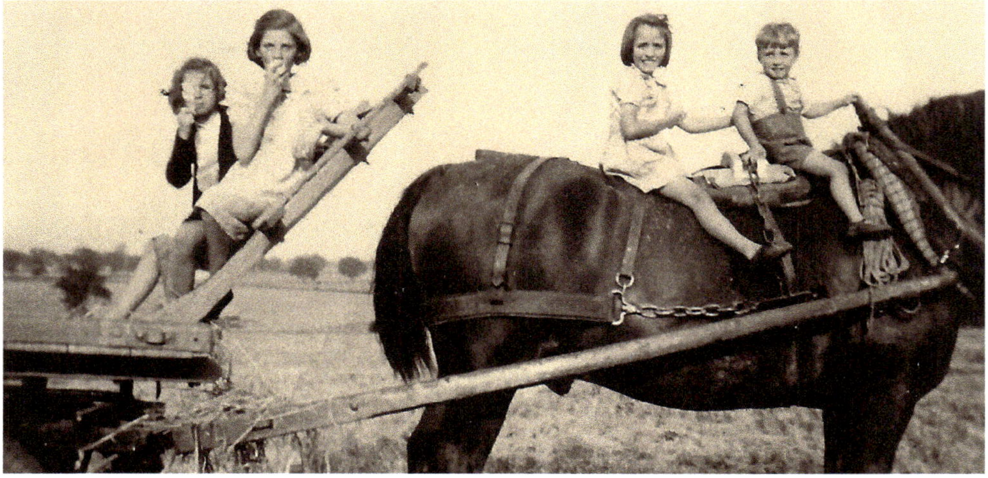

Pearl Burroughs (Wisbey) with her brother Conrad at harvest.

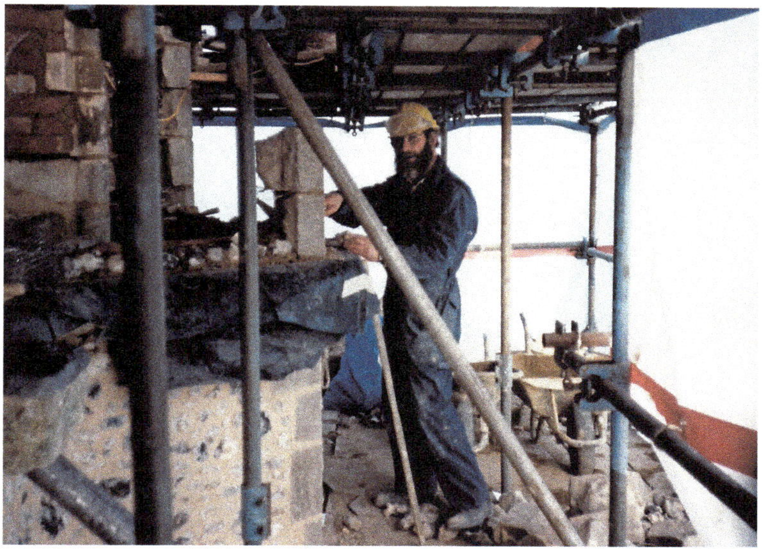

Ron West at work in 1993.

Church Work

I came up to Great Barton in 1948 from Hampshire with my parents. Mother's health wasn't too clever and Dad's new job as a nurseryman was going to allow him more time with her. However things didn't work out and he lost his job after two years. As our home was a tied cottage we were re-housed in the old POW Nissen huts on Hardwick Heath for two years before being offered a council house on Mildenhall Estate. I went to the St Edmunds Roman Catholic School until 1957, leaving to work at Lawsons Electrical on Cornhill for two years; then as a storeman for Botwoods Garage before getting itchy feet. I saw a bricklaying course advertised in the Labour Exchange and went on that. After I finished training in 1967, I worked for H. G. Frost for several years before coming self-employed. There's hardly a street in Bury I haven't worked in at different times. I did a lot of work for F Valiant & Son who specialised in church work. Over lunch once, with my mate Jim Farr we counted over sixty churches we had worked on in Suffolk. While working for a Braintree firm, I turned up for work on a Monday morning at West Stow church and asked my then mate to load up the hoist with flints and mortar for the work ahead of us. He came back to me and said, 'it aint there, somebody's nicked the hoist'. I couldn't believe it especially when the vicar lived opposite and was about the whole weekend and saw nothing! I can also remember working on Castle Camps church near Haverhill when a roofer found a bottle with the names of workers who had worked on the church roof twenty years previously. We fished the piece of paper out of the bottle and added ours to the bottom, agreeing with the message which said, 'This was a dirty, filthy job', meaning the roof. We put the bottle back for some future generation to find. I now enjoy going out with the Bury St Edmunds Ramblers and re-visiting some of the churches I once worked on.

Ron West (born 1942).

Appreciative of Bury St Edmunds

My wife Barbara had grandparents who lived in Glemsford so as a young child she knew Bury quite well. My childhood was spent loving architecture inspired by my art teacher. This love led me to study at the School of Architecture qualifying as an architect in 1951. Luckily I was deferred from National Service so I could finish my exams before going into the RAF. Can you believe it I was put into the Airfield Construction Branch, what luck! I can remember being sent into the Suez Canal Zone and while there one Christmas I sat down to eat 'Desert Chicken and Whistleberries', corn beef and dried peas! After my service I went back to work as an architect but was made redundant after six months eventually working in several private practices. I succeeded in getting a job for an international oil company working on mainly planning matters till I retired. In the 1970s my wife and I holidayed in Bury several times. We were living in the Borough of Epsom and Ewell in Surrey then; I was also an independent councillor there. In 1980, we purchased a house in Westgate Street as a second home. We joined the Bury Society as we believed in integrating with the local community; I was later to become its chairman. During my period as chairman, the society was opposed to the moving of the Cattle Market up onto Rougham Hill the first of two schemes, we all know what happened to the second with the demise of livestock markets everywhere! In 1987 my early retirement led us to buy a new house in College Street on the site of the old workhouse infirmary. I have always appreciated history and became an archaeological volunteer and went on to write a small book entitled 'Riches and Rags', basically a history of the workhouse and its site. I was once asked where you would like to live. My reply was, 'I'm already there - Bury St Edmunds'. It has all the facilities you could ever want and as you get older living in the town centre the need for a car diminishes.

Peter Plumridge (born 1929).

Conflicts

Being Prepared

When war came I was attending the Feoffment, all the widows there were sandbagged and if an air raid sounded we were to go into the underground part of the brewery. The school caretaker would give me some hot water for my Oxo cube, which I had for dinner as there was no canteen. One particular day the school was closed as it might be used as a possible casualty post for the air-borne troops going to Arnhem. There were lots of these troops around the town then and I saw gliders being towed in the air over Bury. I learnt about Arnhem later on. Locally the army prepared for any invasion by having large concrete blocks ready to shut off the road as underneath the railway bridge in Eastgate Street, where the A14 flyover is now. The bridge carried the line to Sudbury and a concrete pill box was built near to it; some poor chap died in its construction! At the back of the houses in Eastgate Street soldiers unrolled concertina barbed wire and up by Hollow Road where we lived there was a tank trap. Times were hard then and my mother used to buy a shillings worth of meat with her ration coupons but also eked it out with a pennyworth of corn beef, I suppose everybody else had to do something similar. Later in life I went on to join the Royal Engineers following my father and other family members, serving for twelve years then a further fourteen years in the TA.

Michael Robertson (born 1932).

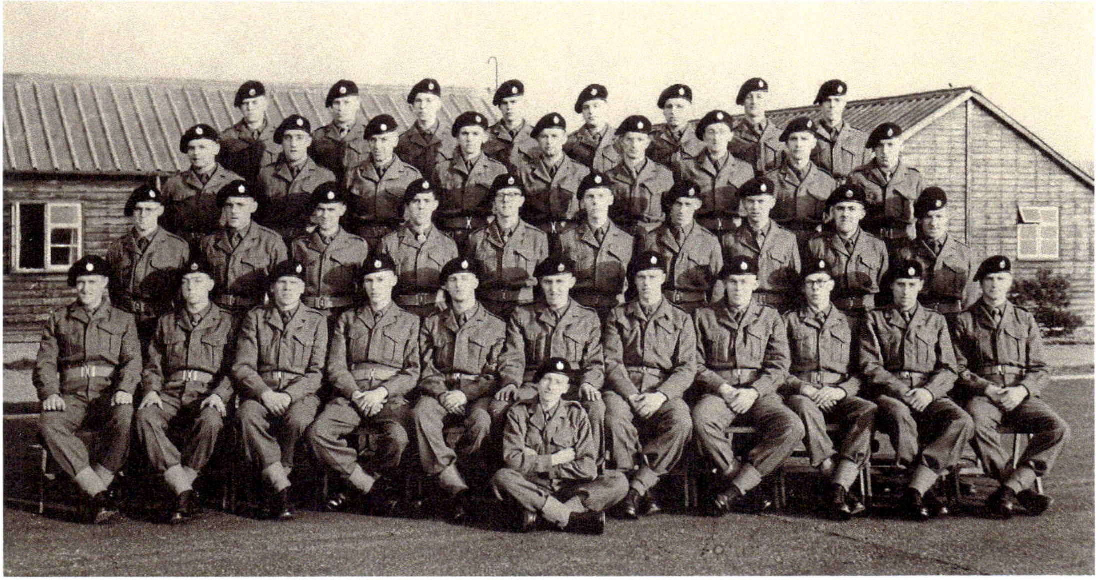

Michael Robertson, third from left front row, in the Royal Engineers.

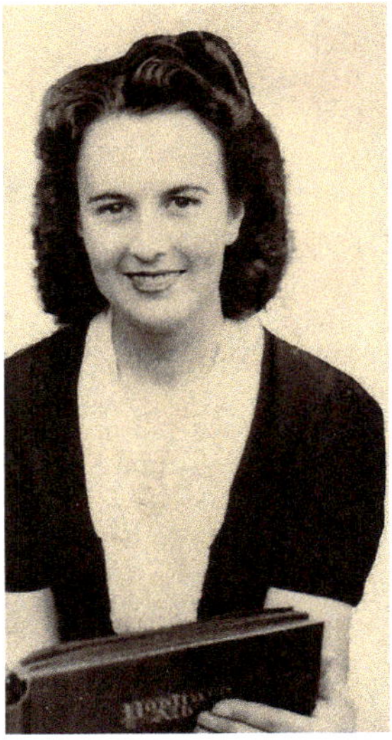

Eileen Fuller (Tooke), a smooth dancer.

Hurricanes

Just before I was called up in the Second World War the air raid siren went and a single German plane went overhead, we all just made it to the shelter not knowing if it was going to drop bombs on us! After basic training at Letchworth I was sent to Witney in Oxfordshire to work on Hurricane tail planes at the De Havilland factory. I was billeted in a B&B in the town a twenty-five minute walk from the factory but didn't wear a uniform. I liked going to dances in Witney Town Hall and met my first husband Ellis there, he was a Mosquito pilot. We moved back to Bury in 1953 living in Albert Crescent, Hardwick Lane and Queens Road. I went on to work for Marks & Spencer for twenty years. Sadly Ellis died at an early age in 1968.

Eileen Fuller (formerly Jennings) Née Tooke (born 1920).

Rationing

I was aged fourteen when I got my first job, earning five shillings a week at County Electrical Services in St Andrew's St South near the corner with Kings Road. I started at 8.30 a.m. in the morning and finished at 5.30 p.m. and had to work Saturday mornings! Out of my paltry pay I was stopped 2*d*. I hated spiders and there were lots of them there! Eventually I was getting paid ten shillings weekly because I helped with the wages. However when war broke out things definitely improved for me as I got a job at the Ministry of Food at the town hall (now Market Cross). My wages doubled to one pound a week! One of my tasks was to make sure any unclaimed ration books issued at The Corn Exchange were taken down to the police station where they were locked in a cell as they were very valuable. Once a policeman pulled my leg (I hoped) and threatened to lock me up with them as well! I can still remember my ration book number, it was TYAM/3.

Gwen Brunskill née Cockle (born1923).

Medal Presentation

After I enlisted in the Royal Air Force I trained at Hereford during 1959/60 before ending up in 1962 at RAF Honington. My job wasn't very glamourous, I worked in the stores, later I got posted to Borneo and spent twelve months there. Do you know what? I got a campaign medal for that. I was called to the CO's Admin Block one day and went into an office where a clerk was sitting, he chucked this medal onto the desk and said, 'That's yours, off you go!' No ceremony or nothing! After I married in 1966 my wife and I were stationed in Penang, Malaya for two years before coming back to Suffolk. I came out of the RAF in 1974.

Malcolm Cannell (born 1944).

Following Dad

In the Second World War at the bottom of Petticoat Lane where the BP fuel station is now (2015), there was a mortar emplacement manned by the Home Guard. Basically a 5-foot-deep pit with a short concrete pillar in the middle, on which sat a mortar on a stainless steel spigot. We were then living in Vinery Road having moved from the Priors Estate. Like everybody else we had an Anderson air-raid shelter in the back garden. The POWs from Hardwick came by our house in open top lorries on the way to work in farmer's fields. Because Rougham Airfield wasn't too far away whenever there was a plane crash we used to get on our bikes and get to the crash site and try to retrieve something, if you could get a piece of Perspex you had done well. My father Bertie who was born in 1897 enlisted at seventeen becoming a dispatch rider in France. He was in the home guard during WW2. It was his love of motor cycling that I followed at the age of fifteen, I even when to France on my motorbike after the end of the war to follow in Dad's footsteps. That was my first taste of travelling abroad, something I have enjoyed ever since.

Brian Ransome (born 1934).

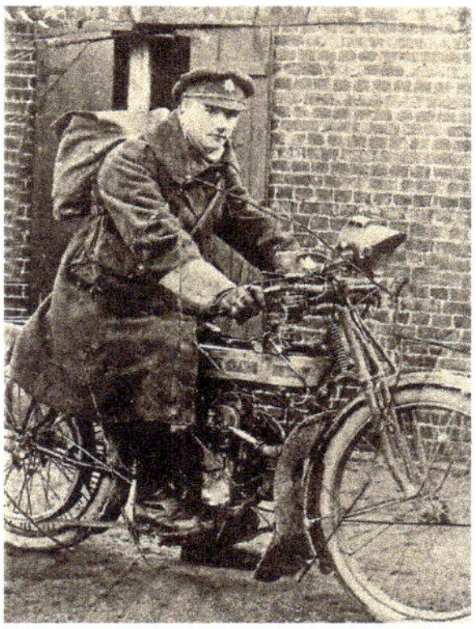

Bertie Ransome WW1 Dispatch Rider.

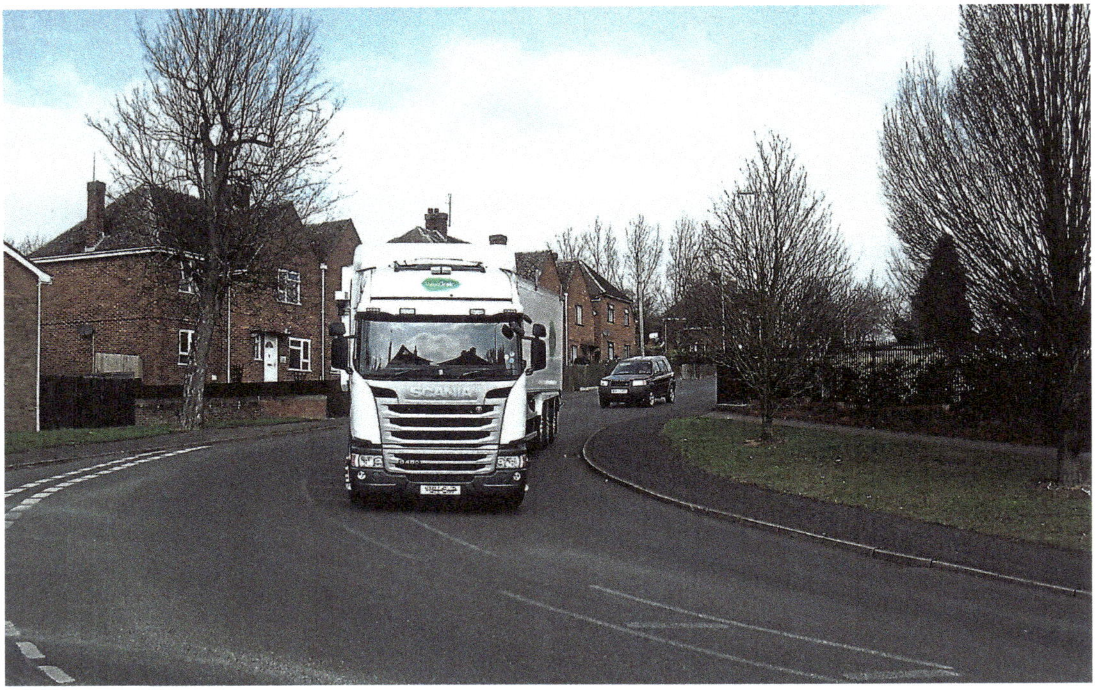

The much-altered bend, bottom of West Road AKA Cemetery Hill.

A Steep Hill

My father was a solicitor in the town and we lived at No. 91, Hospital Road, a bungalow facing West Road a steep hill with a sharp bend, much altered since. Our fence was demolished by conveys during the war careering down the hill. During one incident a truck towing its trailer lost its load, a large bomb! The driver asked mother if he could use the phone to report what had happened, he was lucky as not everyone was on the phone then. Mother went outside to offer another chap a cup of tea and saw him sitting astride the bomb lighting his fag. Startled she said 'should you be doing that', he replied in an American accent re-assuring her 'don't worry Mam it aint primed!' Once an Italian POW came a cropper on his bike into our fence; he said in broken English 'not a good hill to come down with no brakes!' He asked for something to straighten his forks and wheel and then went on his way. A couple of weeks later a man knocked on the door and when Mother answered it was given two little silver aeroplanes made from a beaten florin (2*s* piece). The rather nice Italian man said they were for the little boys, meaning my brother and me. Once mother saw some chaps digging the other side of our fence at the bottom of our garden. When she asked what they were doing they replied 'This is the second line of defence'. Mother just said 'well, what side are we on?' I can just about remember the end of war celebrations in the Abbey Gardens. At one stall you paid for three darts to throw at a picture of Hitler that worried me no end.

Ted Ashton (born 1941).

Living in Cullum Road

Five generations of the Ridgeon family lived in Cullum Road for well over a hundred years; a residential home is near there now. The Butts was just like living in the countryside but at the top of Cullum Road there were all sorts of shops, you didn't need to go into the town centre for anything! When the war came my father put up blackout frames on the windows, not too hard as we only had four. He worked as a plate layer on the now defunct Bury to Sudbury railway line and obtained the odd rabbit that strayed too close to the line if you know what I mean! Rationing was tough on my mother, like everyone else she did the best she could with what she had. She would make the most marvellous scrambled eggs from the powdered egg! I heard a lot of people discussing the war but I was very confused by it all. At my first school, St Peters Infants my earliest memory is the disappointment at having to play a triangle instead of a tambourine! We celebrated Empire day back then. I liked watching the women who wove camouflage netting on the 'Bungy' the sloping forecourt that leads up to the Hunter Club (2015).

David Ridgeon (born 1932).

Bluebells

During September 1944, there were lots of troops around in Bury. We had some billeted with us. However, some of them upset my father one day by taking down our wooden gate to use on a fire. My mother smoothed over the situation by baking some scones, a case of forgive and forget. Dad was in the Home Guard which used to meet at the Sugar Beet factory so knew a little bit of what was going on, preparation for Arnhem. One day, a doodlebug went over Bury and landed somewhere in Hengrave. My father managed the woods there and went to investigate, a scene of devastation; it would be a long time before we could go and see the bluebells again; something we always enjoyed doing.

Bridget James née Reynolds (born 1936).

Respectable soldiers

During the war, we lived in Grove Park and had four friendly soldiers billeted with us. We knitted socks for them. I was allowed to go to dances at the Barracks at fourteen as I was escorted home. One of them said that when his mother died he would come back to Bury as he liked it so much, and he did. He became a friend for life. I can also remember Dad being in the Observer Corps during the war. Every Sunday I used to get a bottle of beer from the Falcon. I would take it with some food that Mum had made to Westley Airfield where Dad and his mate Charlie Bonner were on duty. Charlie was an auctioneer at Lacey Scott.

Gwen Roberts née Pawsey (born 1931).

It Was Expected of Me

I was promised after my National Service a place at Cambridge University to study law so on completion of my basic training I went off to Korea in late December 1952. I was commissioned as a 2nd Lieutenant and saw six months active service there, on occasions having shells rain down over my head. I did everything that was expected of me. I came back to England; the war finished in July 1953 and I went off to Cambridge in September of 1954. After three years there I became an articled clerk in Norwich for another three. After I qualified in 1960, I went to work for Bankes Ashton Solicitors then on the corner of Abbeygate Street and Guildhall Street with a weekly wage of £13 10*s*. I did virtually everything and anything that was expected of me! After the firm moved around the corner into No. 81, Guildhall Street I specialised in criminal and matrimonial law working within the firm eventually becoming a partner. Since I retired I have enjoyed the company of so many people in Bury which is a wonderful friendly place.

Jos Bird (Born 1933).

Holiday Camp

I did my two-year stint National Service in the Royal Artillery being posted to Cyprus; it was just like a holiday camp! I became a lance-bombadier and participated in the regimental pentathalon team as I was quite good at sports in general. Later on I went on to play for Bury Rugby Club.

Kingsley Curtis (born 1937).

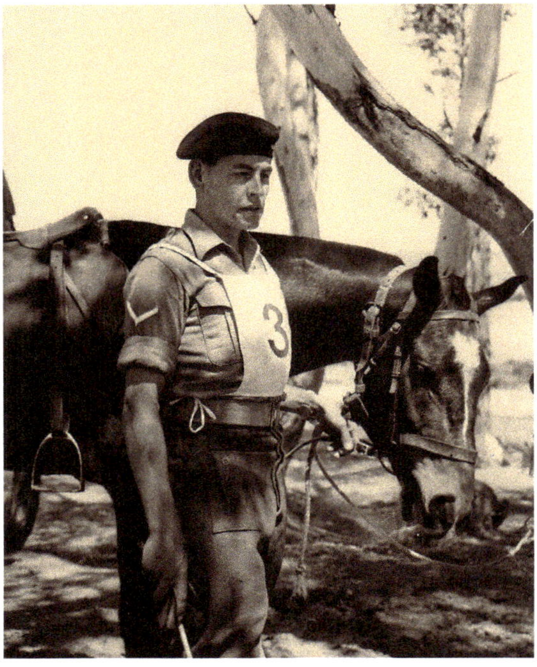

Lance Bombadier Kingsley Curtis participating in the regimental pentathalon.

Nearly in the Korean War

When I was eighteen I got called up joining the Suffolk Regiment. I did six weeks of basic training at the barracks then another four at Blenheim Camp. The Korean War was raging and I fully expected to go but my age was not quite right so I never went with the Suffolks. I volunteered with nine others to join the Essex Regt, which was the next lot to go to Korea. The journey took six weeks going via Gibraltar, The Med, Port Said, Aden, Colombo, Singapore and finally Hong Kong. The war was finishing so we never got to see any action but it was an amazing experience. I came home to England in November 1955.

Bill Pattle (born 1935).

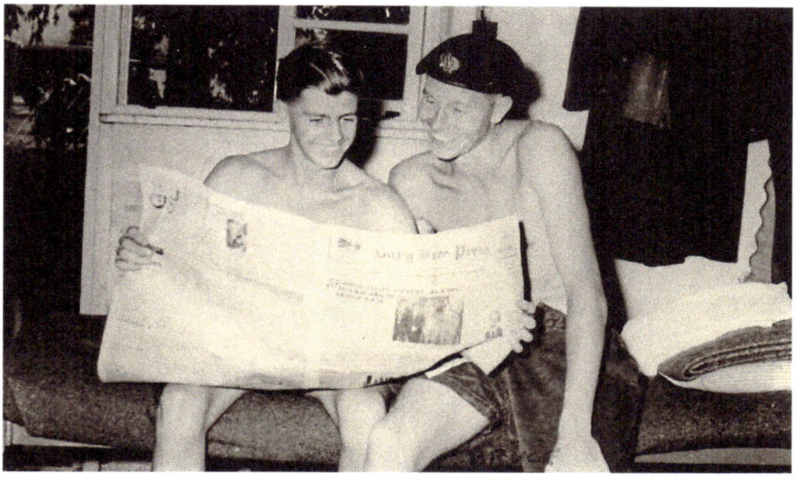

Bill Pattle sharing the *Bury Free Press* sent to him by his mother.

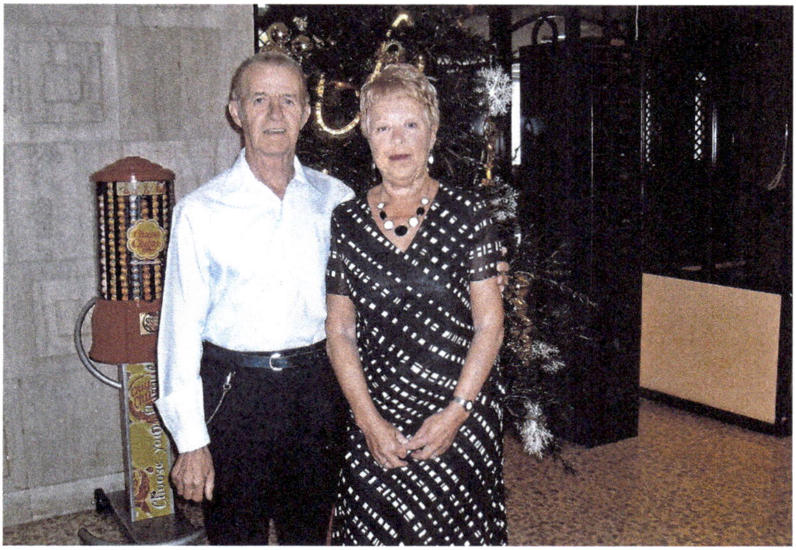

Bill and Shirley Pattle enjoying a night out.

Entertaining the Troops

My father went into the Royal Engineers when I was seven years old. I was at the Feoffment School then and all us children had to do practices with gas masks. We lived on the corner of Looms Lane and Northgate Street, the house has since been demolished. A woman and her young daughter were billeted with us; this woman's husband was away in the army. My mother had a knock on the front door one night and there stood an American military policeman. He asked my mother if the lodger could keep her window locked as American GIs were seen climbing through to be 'entertained' on occasions. Mum was most indignant!

Daphne Elliston née Warren (born 1932).

Splice the Mainbrace

I joined the Royal Navy in 1942 serving as a stoker on the *King George V* which was inspected by the King and Queen before setting off for the Pacific. As they left, the order was given to 'splice the mainbrace', the rum ration being doled out! When I crossed the equator for the first time I was presented with a framed certificate known as 'Domain of Neptunus Rex'. As I worked down in the 'stoke hole' I never got to see any action but I remember one day the padre giving us a running commentary when we were attacked by kamikazes, very worrying that! When we arrived in Tokyo for the Japanese surrender I was one of a shore party sent to reopen the British Embassy. We saw loads of Japanese crying and throwing themselves on the ground, some even committing Hari-Kari as they couldn't believe their Emperor had surrendered. Back at our ship I attended one of the hospital ships with our lads who had been POWs; they were in a sorry state. One of them asked me to write a letter to his mum and dad which I did and later got a lovely thank you letter back which I still have.

Spencer Derek Bluett (born 1925).

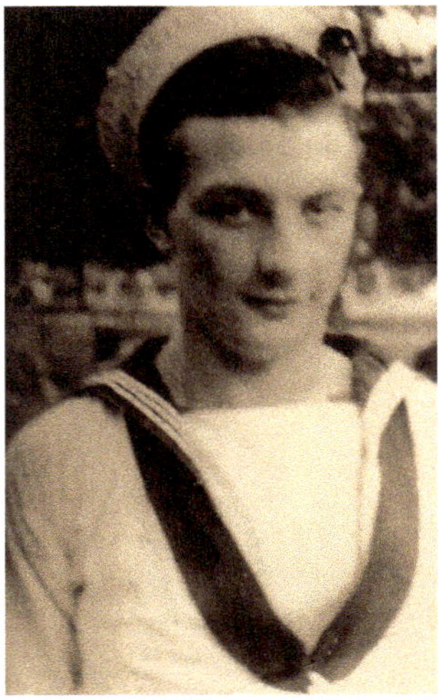

Seaman Spencer Derek Bluett.

A German POW Story

I was called up for the Wehrmacht in 1940 and joined the 23rd Tank Division receiving two war injuries. It was while I was in Normandy in 1944 that I was captured by the Americans and taken to Cherbourg. There were two ships waiting to take POWs to Southampton, one newly painted the other not so. I said to my friend 'let's get on the old one as it was less likely to get bombed by the Germans!' In England I alternated between a small camp at Drinkstone and Bury before settling down at the camp at Hardwick. I went to several farms in the area; one at Boxted near Glemsford was where I had to get up at 5 a.m. in the morning to milk forty cows. I was asked whether I would help with the harvest, I said no thanks as we only got paid camp money for use in the canteen there. The beer wasn't too bad here providing you strained it first! When working for Mr Gittus the farmer, I was told along with others to pick up all the potatoes in the field before the tractor and trailer returned. Once he said to me 'How come you Germans always finish before those Italians?' I was in Tilbury when the war finished but came back to Bury in 1947, although I wasn't allowed the freedom out of the camp until a year later when I could go into town. I got to know Mr Taylor, the hairdresser next to the Odeon, and via him acquired an American serviceman's jacket which I dyed in an old tin bath. With the help of a Mrs Hawkins, I then got a ladies long coat, gave it to George the tailor at the camp and he made a smart pair of trousers from it for me. I was then able to walk about town unrecognisable as a POW until one lady came up to me and said, 'I know you, you're one of them POW's'. That lady was Vera Brettell who went to dances with me at the Co-op Hall and later became my wife. After we married I worked at Hawkins Fish & Chip shop in Brentgovel, Street eventually owning my own shop in Risbygate Street. Everyone came to know me as John.

Johann Hopfensberger (born 1923).

Tears

During the war we had three soldiers billeted at my father's pub, The Spread Eagle. We also had the Home Guard and the Army practise manoeuvres in the area. One day a soldier let off a tear gas canister in the dry linnet bed right under my mother's kitchen window. It nearly filled the place, our poor cat's eyes streaming and when the regulars came in for their pint, theirs as well! The officer in charge apologised but mother called him everything under the sun!

Ron Colson (born1929).

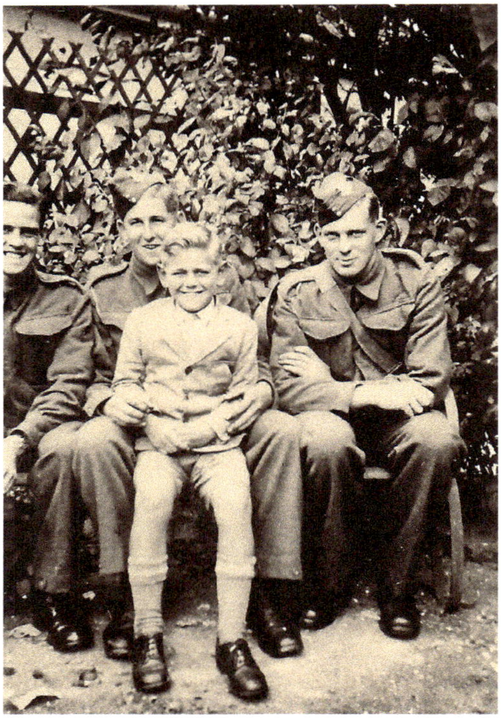

A young Ron Colson with billeted soldiers.

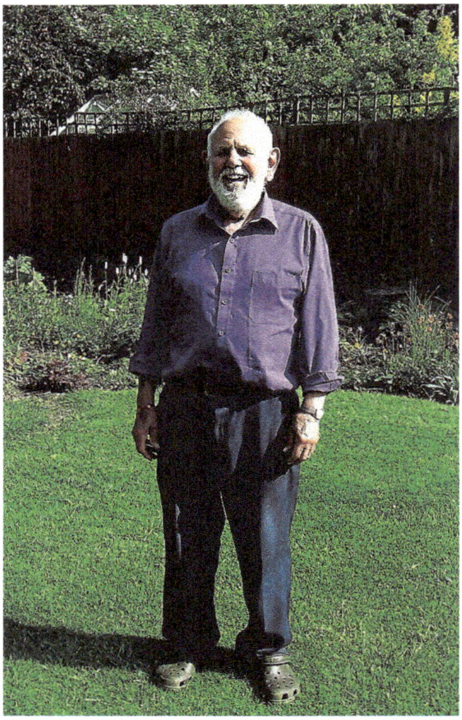

Ron Colson in his more senior years, 2015.

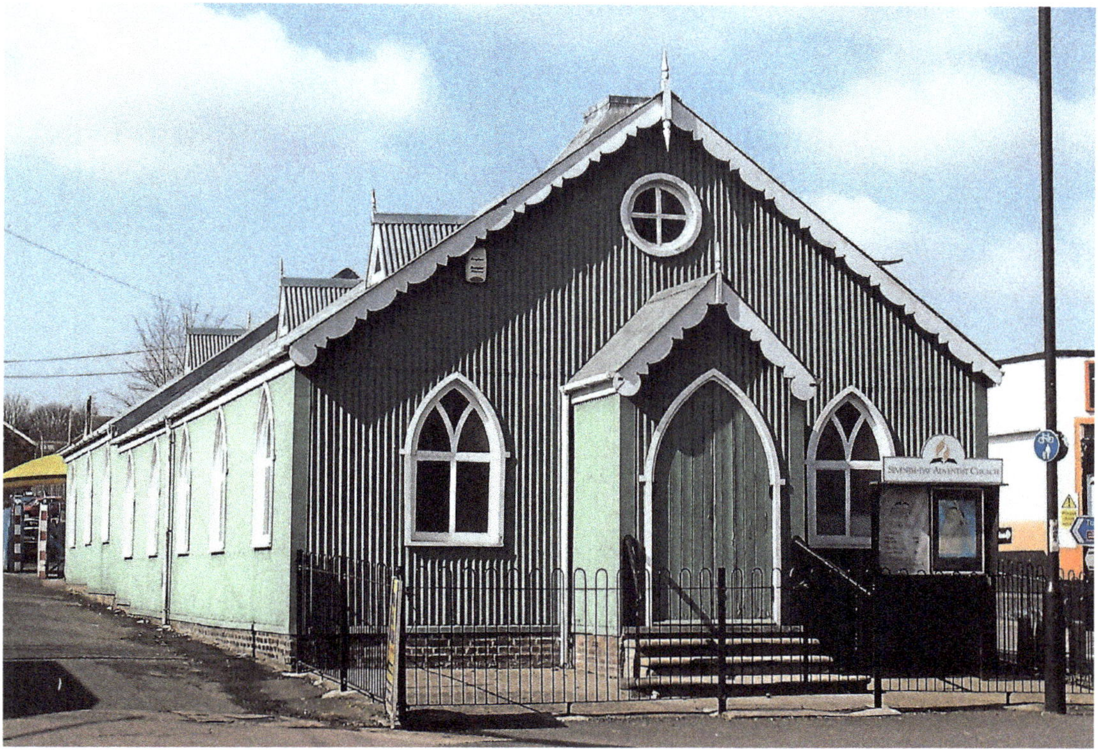

Once the Railway Mission Hall now the Seventh Day Adventist church in Fornham Road.

Rum Work

Wartime Bury was much the same for everyone else. During the war there was double summertime, clocks being put forward two hours allowing farmers to get the harvest in. Towards the end of the war I can remember German POWs from Fornham coming to the Railway Mission Hall in Fornham Road and singing to us as a choir! I left school at fifteen; the leaving age had just been put up from fourteen. I worked at Burlinghams Mill on Station Hill before getting my call-up papers. I joined the RAF and could have gone in just for two years but worked it out that going in for three meant better pay, more leave and other benefits. I hadn't been married very long to my wife Gloria when she became very ill preventing me from going to Korea. This was in 1953, the year of the dreadful floods around the East coast. I was stationed then at Bawdsey and helped during the day and into the early evening filling sandbags for the sea defences there. The 'Sally Army' looked after us and in the continuous pouring rain a much appreciated half bottle of rum was added to the tea urn. Prince Philip turned up to thank everyone for their hard work, the trouble was most of those who had been doing it, us, were tucked up in bed shattered!

Ivan Abbott (born 1933).

Twins

My father was one of a pair of twins, his name was John French Addy and his brother was Horace Dorrien Addy, both named after the First World War generals! The twins were born in December 1914 in Kent. My father did several rural jobs like charcoal burning and working on farms, he even worked for Kent County Council painting the white lines on the roads! In around 1938, he joined up as a dispatch rider in the Royal Corps of Signals. During the war his unit was posted to Bury and was based on the corner of Southgate Street and Maynewater Lane. He was billeted at No. 2, Southgate Street, where he met my mum, Pamela Petit, who lived there.

David Addy (born 1948).

First Oranges

My father was a clerk at Greene King and also in The Suffolk Mounted Yeomanry. He was called up and went straight off to France. We had moved from Victoria Street to Priors Avenue just before then. Rationing was on; we got our meat from Fulchers the butchers in St John's Street and groceries from Olivers in Abbeygate Street. All dairy produce like butter, cheese and margarine had to be weighed out and wrapped up in brown paper. There was no such thing as bananas or oranges. Near the end of the war, the shop girl there saved my mother two oranges for my brother and me, what a treat. Greene King looked after their staff that had gone off to war, that enabled me to go from the Convent School to the King Edward Grammar Prep School. I was six then, staying at the Grammar school till I was seventeen. After father got back from Dunkirk, he was posted off to Bournemouth and we as a family went down to see him by train that kept stopping because of air raids. We were with him a whole week. As children we stood at the bottom of West Road waving to American trucks to slow down because of the bend, they threw gum and sweeties to us as a thank you.

John Abbott (born 1935).

Flying from Rougham

My early life was in Sicklesmere; my grandfather had a haulage company and undertakers business there. The Americans stationed at Rougham Airfield came to the Sicklesmere Rushbrooke Arms for a drink and I got friendly with them. I had joined the Army cadets and if I wore my uniform I was allowed onto the base; while there I was asked if I wanted to go up, cor did I! Altogether I had three flights, one over East Anglia, another to Ireland where I was violently sick because of bad weather and the last in a Flying Fortress over Germany dropping leaflets. The war was over by then. When VJ day came, the pubs in the Sicklesmere area had celebration bottles of beer. My uncle 'Oweny' Plumb and his mate got the contract to deliver them to the various local pubs starting at The Fox & Hounds at Bradfield. By the time they got to the last one, The Metcalf Arms at Hawstead they were absolutely sloshed. I had to drive the lorry home, still only fourteen!

Fred Roberts (born 1931).

Our Wartime

When I was twenty-one I was called up and went to work in a factory near London making aircraft parts on a lathe, it was boring work. My sister Joan was not called up as she had married her husband John in 1943, although she did volunteer work as a fire watcher. Joan's husband John came from Cheshire and was billeted in Bury when she met him. He was in the Royal Army Service Corps and she can still remember his army number, No. 223250! After the war, he went to work at Nice & Co. as a coach trimmer. My husband Harry 'John' whom I had known for a long time was in the Territorials and joined the Royal Artillery; he was at Dunkirk and North Africa. Post-war he went back to working for Shell. When the war ended me and Joan went up to London for the celebrations with our young brother Brian, we ended up sleeping on the kerb in The Strand!

Betty Woodward née Ransome (born 1921).
Joan Horsham née Ransome (born 1923).

Story of a POW

My husband Edward, or 'Ted' as he was always known, was born in 1917 in Blyth, Northumberland. He came down with his dad to see relatives, the Hammonds who kept a shop in Risbygate Street where they sold among other goods, cigarettes and tobacco. When the war came he enlisted in the Royal East Kent Regiment, known as the 'Buffs'. Going over to France he was caught up in the rear guard action to hold up the German army from getting to Dunkirk to prevent the evacuation. He was captured and spent the rest of the war as a POW in Stalag 17. While there he wrote a letter to his brother not knowing that he was dead. He learnt to speak fluent German and when the war ended was asked to work as an interpreter for the American Army. He reckoned he had done his bit and 'politely' refused! He came back to live in Risbygate Street and met me. He was just sixty two when he died.

Gwen Brunskill née Cockle (born 1923).

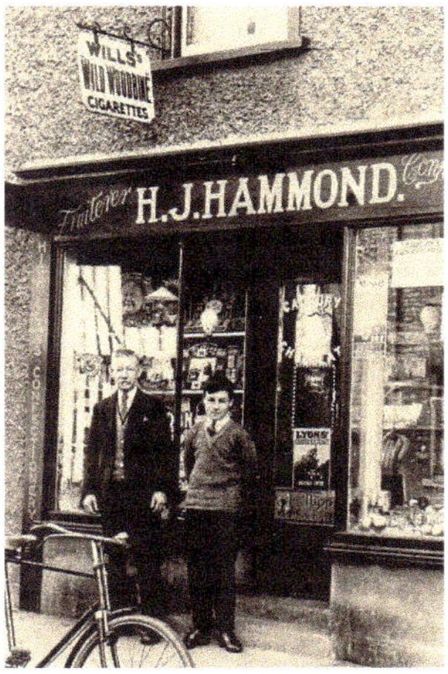

Hammond's Stores and Tobacconists at 31, Risbygate Street.

Cheese

I used to go over to Rougham airfield; the American soldiers were always very smartly turned out. During 1944 there were thousands of soldiers in tents up by the East Anglian School, I later found out they were probably waiting for D-Day. The soldiers were very generous, once an American soldier gave me what looked like an orange sweet, it wasn't; it was the first time I tasted orange cheese! One day during 1945 up by 'The Chalks' (rear of station) I heard an almighty thump above my head, two of our planes had collided. I saw a parachute open and the planes go into the sugar beet factory slurry pits. The next day I went down there and saw a lone parachute dangling from a dead tree, the poor airman had probably drowned. I used to go up to Hardwick Heath where the POW camp was, they obviously had no intention of escaping as the soldiers patrolled from inside the fence! During my National Service from 1954–56, I wanted to join the RAF but missed my interview in Cambridge as the train was delayed, so I ended up in the Royal Artillery. After basic training I thought I was going to be posted away somewhere but was told to report to Woolwich Arsenal for a special secondment. I ended up in Berkeley Square; the upshot of it was that I worked for The Adjutant General's Department. I quickly rose from gunner to sergeant within this classified unit wearing civvies instead of my uniform and put into digs in Kilburn, earning the enormous sum then of thirteen guineas a week! Returning to Bury after my spell away was like chalk and cheese, from the high life of London to the sedate pace of life here took some adjusting. Eventually I got a job with Post Office Telephones and via evening classes and correspondence courses worked my way up the ladder ending up in management at BT, retiring at fifty-five.

Gerald 'Gerry' Travers (born 1935).

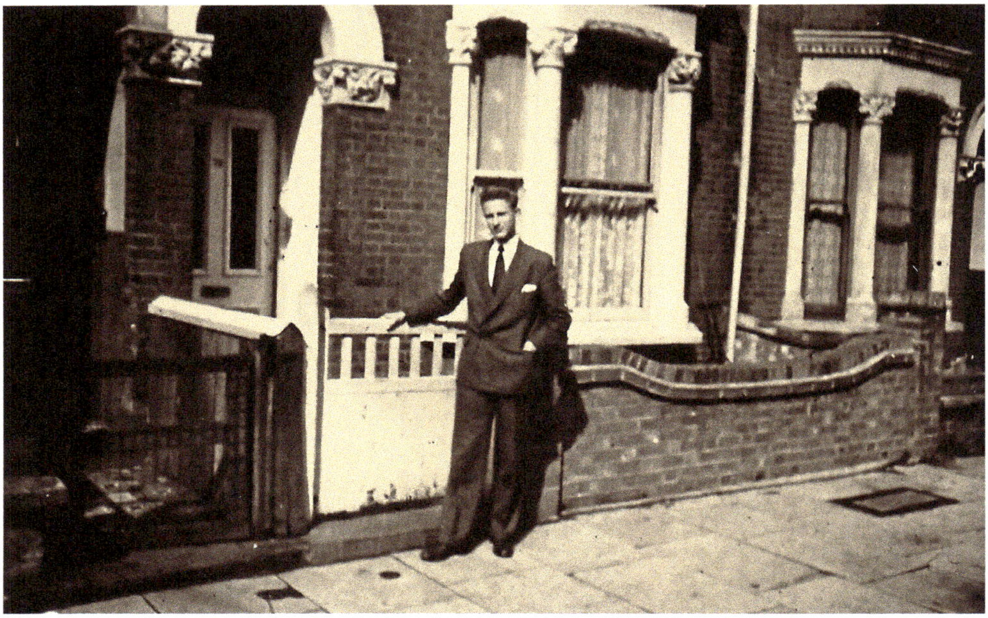

Gerry Travers outside his digs in Kilburn, London.

French Canadians

My home for about eleven years was in Guildhall Street. During the war, we were issued with gas masks at the British Legion but I was never frightened. Whenever a plane crashed, boys used to get a souvenir like a piece of shrapnel, only years later did I find out what that word actually meant! By the way parachute silk was highly collectable. During the Second World War, we had two great aunts stay with us for three years. My father had scooped them up from Worthing and brought them to Bury for safety. He worked shifts and weekends at the Hand Laundry, which he and my mother owned. He had a reserved occupation for the war effort, troop work it was called! One night when he was working, there was a knock on the door. My uncle answered it and there stood two good-looking uniformed soldiers who spoke French. Because our house had two small doors they assumed we were a pub and wanted to come in. Uncle told them to clear off or he would set the dogs on them. Sure enough our two 'vicious' spaniels flew down the stairs and lay down at their feet! Fortunately, the two chaps realised their error, smiled and left much to the disappointment of my mother and her sister.

Sheila Bayne née Forbes (born 1938).

The Midnight Coalman

Albert Sharman acquired this nickname due to his inability to get up in the mornings, always completing his deliveries late at night. He had a coal yard in Toper Lane just off Raingate Street but would collect his coal from coal wagons on Station Hill. At the top of this hill was a weighbridge owned by Ridleys Coal & Iron Co. A story went that Albert and his father once weighed themselves on here, the result being over a quarter of a ton! During the war, Albert was doing one of his nocturnal deliveries in Eastgate Street in his horse-drawn cart. Its rear red light was not seen by an American serviceman who drove into the back of it. Albert managed to get a replacement cart from my father but it had O. Childs, Bakers on it. My father got ribbed that he was venturing into the coal business. Anyway father sent an employee called Fred to paint out the sign. Fred was a handyman called on to do various things, it was said he would get a pound of nails from Andrews & Plumptons to complete the job. The upshot of it all was that Fred went down to Albert's yard and painted out O. Childs in bright green paint but left Bakers and Corn Merchant and the telephone number!

Anthony Childs (born 1932).

Ham for Tea

My mum was a housewife, dad a furniture dealer, he was called up before I was born in Hollow Road. When the air raid sirens sounded me and several other small kids would get on our trikes and pedal as fast as we could as we were frightened. Our parents used to grab hold of us and run to the shelter at the back of Chapmans Café opposite the sugar beet factory. On one bombing raid a German bomber did manage to hit one of the nearby houses killing someone. They were trying to destroy the bridge over the east coast railway, one crater was only a few yards from the line! American bombers used to take off from Rougham disappearing over the horizon. One horrible incident I can remember was an airborne collision between two planes resulting in a body lying in Hollow Road, my mother hastily pulled me away to stop me from looking at it. Although I was very young, I still can see it today in my mind's eye as if it was yesterday. After the war, German POWs had to fill in the tank trap that extended from the beet factory, past Charlie Flack's farm and out to Great Barton rail crossing. We kids used to help them, they were clever blokes that made figures from chalk and wove baskets that they sold. Something else they also sold was the ham from their sandwiches, ham being scarce and not available to the locals. With the money the POWs bought cigarettes. Over the course of a year one of them called Hans befriended the gang of seven kids I belonged to. On the day he was sent back home he waved goodbye at us with his white handkerchief as we stood on Hollow Road bridge. One of my favourite memories is of 'Nana' Chapman at the café. She would sell teas, rolls and cakes to the beet lorry drivers. At the end of the day she would give us any leftover doughnuts. The trouble was we grew to expect them turning up earlier and earlier for our very welcome treat. Eventually she got fed up and told us to clear off!

Keith Steed (born 1942).

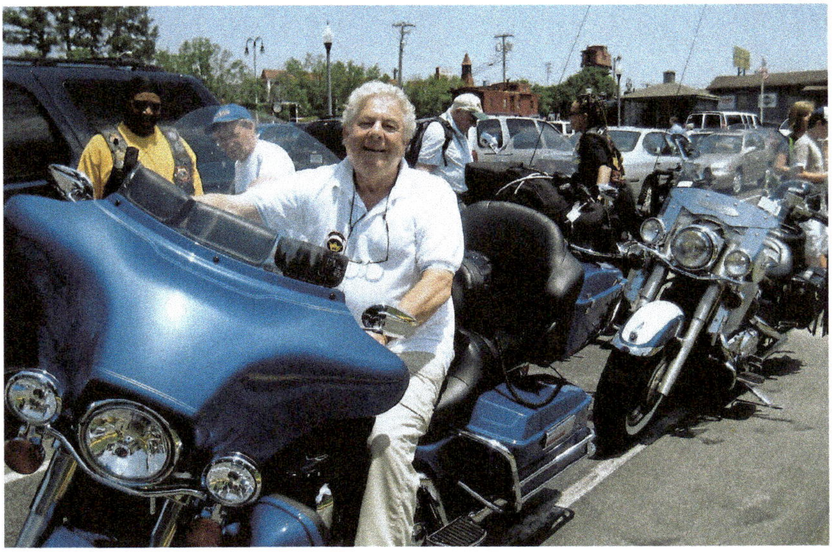

Keith Steed, no longer riding a trike!